GREEN FEASTS

Richard Cawley
Green Feasts
Memorable Meat-free Menus

Photography by
Debbie Patterson

Conran Octopus

For Joan Campbell

Unless stated otherwise, all menus and recipes serve 6 people.
Metric and imperial measures are both given in the recipes in this
book, use one or the other as the two are not interchangeable. Spoon
measurements are level unless otherwise stated.

Editorial Direction: Lewis Esson Publishing
Art Direction: Mary Evans
Design: Alison Fenton
Food for Photography: Richard Cawley with Ian Hands; Jane
Suthering
Editorial Assistant: Penny David
Production: Mano Mylvaganam

First published in 1993 by
Conran Octopus Limited,
37 Shelton Street,
London WC2H 9HN

British Library Cataloguing in Publication Data
A catalogue record for this book is available from the British Library

ISBN 1-85029-455-0

Typeset by Servis Filmsetting Ltd, Manchester, U.K.
Printed and bound by Wing King Tong Co Ltd, Hong Kong

CONTENTS

LIST OF MENUS

THE BREADWINNER 80

Radishes and Corn Wafers with Three Pâtés

Savoury Bread and Butter Pudding
Seasonal vegetables
Fresh Figs with Rum and Mascarpone

FARMER'S BASKET 86

Caponata

Gratin of Eggs with Smothered Onions and
    Roquefort
Basmati rice

Apple Tarts with Calvados Cream Sauce

THE COLOURS OF
SUMMER 92

Tomato and Basil Salad
Rosemary Focaccia

Grilled Polenta with Mushrooms, Artichokes
    and Brie
Green and Orange Salad

Summer Fruit Salad in Pineau des Charentes

PIZZA PARTY 98

Barbecued Vegetable Platter

Pizza of Radicchio, Chèvres, Tomatoes,
    Olives and Capers
Passion Fruit and Pineau Syllabub with
    Burnt Sugar Shards

THREE STAR MEAL 102

Asparagus Mousses with Vegetable Beurre
    Blanc

Gnocchi with Spinach and Peas
Green salad

Australian Apple Chocolate Cake

NEW WORLD
WARMER 106

Refried Beans with Melted Cheese and
    Avocado

Chilli con Funghi and Spoon Bread Pie
Wilted Watercress with Olive Oil and Garlic

New England Apple Shortcakes

FROZEN ASSETS 112

Grilled Goats' Cheese on Corn Bread with
    Mushroom Ragout

Avocado and Walnut Risotto
Very Green Salad with Herb Vinaigrette
Cappuccino Ice-cream

FAST START 116

Danielle's Grilled Gorgonzola in Leaf Parcels

Tart of Stuffed Tomatoes in Pesto Custard
Beetroot, Red Onion and Pine Kernel Salad

Warm Goats' Cheese Mousse with Walnuts
    and Lavender Honey

THE ITALIAN JOB 122

'Sandwiches' of Baked Aubergine with
    Grilled Peppers and Mozzarella

Penne with Goats' Cheese, Spinach, Broad
    Beans and Peas
Orange, Olive and Onion Salad

Tiramisu

LIST OF RECIPES

To enable the reader to create menus of their own, the recipes in the book are set out below categorized by course or occasion. Obviously many dishes may appear in more than one category – and readers may also find their very own uses for dishes which do not appear in our listing.

Unless stated otherwise, each recipe is constructed to serve 6 as a starter, main course or accompaniment etc as it appears in its menu. If the dish is to be used in a different role, quantities may have to be scaled up or down appropriately.

INTRODUCTION

Vegetarianism is undoubtedly growing in this country. People are giving up meat – and even perhaps fish – for different reasons, including moral, ecological and health issues. While this book certainly contains no recipes containing meat or fish, it is not concerned with why anyone might choose a vegetarian diet. Indeed, although this book is filled with recipes acceptable to most vegetarians, it is intended not for vegetarians only but for everyone who loves good food.

Until recently, it was almost impossible for vegetarians to find anything acceptable and palatable to eat on most mainstream restaurant menus – except for the ubiquitous omelette and salad. Times are changing at long last, and many good restaurants now routinely offer vegetarian dishes. More often than not, however, restaurants catering specifically for vegetarians still produce heavy 'brown' food with a surprising emphasis on fat-laden pastries and sugar-filled cakes and puddings. Perhaps as a result of this, vegetarianism is only just beginning to throw off its image of sandals and joss sticks, dry 'nut roasts' and anonymous 'savoury bakes'.

Fashion in food seems nowadays to change almost as quickly as in clothing. How many of us cook a favourite recipe time and time again and then find that a few months later it has been totally dropped from our repertoire? Nevertheless, vegetarian food generally seems to be stuck in the '60s and '70s, whereas non-vegetarian food has moved on to a much lighter, healthier and more varied style of eating. In the same way, many vegetarian cookbooks are still written by authors whose prime interest is in the avoidance of meat and meat products, rather than the love of – and a wish to produce – good food.

Although I am not a vegetarian, I have never been a consumer of large amounts of meat – particularly red meat. In 1986 I wrote a book called *Not Quite Vegetarian* which included reasonable quantities of poultry and fish. Such a strategy is now being universally advised by doctors and nutritionists as part of a healthier lifestyle. However, adopting these recommendations means not just eating less red meat, but also consuming less fat and sugar and much more fresh fruit and vegetables and fibre-rich foods like potatoes, pasta, bread, beans and pulses.

What prompted me to write *Green Feasts* is that, when giving a dinner party nowadays, I often find that at least one of my guests will request to be served no meat at all – and often no fish. To provide a separate menu for vegetarian guests not only makes additional work for the cook, but also makes the guest embarrassingly aware of being the cause of this extra trouble.

The simple answer is to cook such a delicious meatless meal for everyone that no one will mind – or even notice – that they are eating a 'vegetarian' meal.

SOURCES OF INSPIRATION

When I decided to write this book I began to compile a list of possible recipe ideas that might be included, with dishes of every kind – simple and sophisticated, traditional and trendy and inspired by cuisines from all over the world. Unfortunately, my list of ideas soon grew long enough to fill a book in itself so I realized that some kind of editing was necessary. To this end I searched for a particular theme around which to plan the menus.

For the past few years I have been fortunate to spend three to four months of each year travelling and I invariably choose to head south for guaranteed sunshine. Not only do I like the look and the feel of sunshine, but I like what it does to the people who live under it – and, perhaps more importantly, what it does to their food.

I love the flavours of the Mediterranean region – of France, Italy, Greece and Turkey – and I have explored the scenery and food in many parts of these countries over the years. The last few long summers, however, I have spent in a magical French valley on the borders of Provence and the Languedoc. This region of goats' cheese and honey, sunflower fields, vineyards and hillsides covered with aromatic wild herbs and purple-cushioned rows of lavender enchanted me so greatly that I recently bought a house there.

It is in these happy surroundings that I enjoy shopping, cooking and eating almost more than anywhere else in the world – except that is for Australia, where for six Christmases past I have escaped the dreariness of grey northern winters for a month of Mediterranean-style summer 'down under'.

MY ANTIPODEAN MUSE

More than a few quizzical eyebrows have been raised when I extol the virtues of modern Australian cooking. However, such sceptics are people who have never visited that sunny continent and imagine it all to be just like the anodyne soap operas. Certainly, if that is the image of Australia you desire, its not difficult to find. Even I have to admit to enjoying the occasional meat pie and 'tinnie' on the beach from time to time.

However, Sydney and the other cities are full of the most wonderful eating possibilities. Restaurants of every kind serve superb, well-cooked and affordable food. Moreover, home cooks prepare delicious modern food which makes the most of the spectacular variety of top-quality Australian produce. Today's Australian cook also entertains with a style of informal sophistication which would bring sighs of admiration from their European counterparts. (Australians also make friends easily, so you won't have to wait long for the invitations.)

This high standard of home cooking and entertaining owes much to the excellent quality of food journalism in Australia, in particular the food and entertaining pages of *Vogue Australia* publications and the extraordinary talent of their food editor of many years who is, in my opinion, perhaps the best food editor in the world.

Joan Campbell is a brilliant cook and journalist, with a unerring visionary eye for what will be the next trend in food. Joan's food pages – with their sparkling new ideas for things to cook that will both delight and impress your guests, be quick and easy to prepare and, above all, look and taste superb – would rekindle the most jaded of appetites.

Luckily my antipodean muse of many years is now a firm friend, although when it comes to swapping recipes on the telephone I sometimes wish she was the food editor of a magazine somewhat closer to home.

THE COOK'S KITCHEN

Professional chefs are expected to spend many long hours in the kitchens. However, this should not necessarily be the case for home cooks. Cooking should be a pleasure, not a chore. The recipes in this book are therefore as quick and simple as I can make them.

Although it is perfectly possible to cook good food using only a few pans, a sharp knife and a couple of spoons, certain kitchen 'gadgets' are well worth the initial investment. I find two indispensable: the first is a good food processor, which saves hours and hours of boring work – chopping onions or grating breadcrumbs by hand is not very creative and takes up time better spent on something more rewarding. My food processor is a 'Magimix' and it is the one thing I would take to a desert island (it also grates coconut perfectly).

A good wok is invaluable for all kinds of cooking. Mine is my second invaluable kitchen 'assistant'. It is a superb lidded version, made by le Creuset, which is very heavy and – while having the traditional curved interior – is cleverly designed with a flat bottom on the outside so that it will sit comfortably and safely on any heat source.

THE SHOPPING BASKET

Little irritates me more than reading in
the publicity blurb for some fashionable
restaurant that the secret of the chef in
the spotlight is that he 'uses only the
freshest of ingredients in his cooking'.
There is nothing special about that. My
mother has done so for years, as does
anyone who pretends to have the sligh-
test interest in food. Some meats, many
cheeses and, of course, wines certainly
improve with ageing, but fresh vegetables should be just that and there is
nothing else to say on the subject.

You will, however, see that my Basics
section and all the recipes are 'highly
seasoned' with as much information as I
can give on any unusual or interesting
ingredients.

TO THE TABLE

The great thing about almost all vegetarian meals is that you can drink whatever
you fancy without having to worry too
much about matching wine to food.
Obviously, however, a subtle and deli-
cate white wine might be overpowered by
a dish that is either very robust or spicy
and some purists also insist that few
wines taste good with either asparagus or
artichokes.

So take this book into the kitchen and
allow it to help you think positively
about vegetarian food. Its contents are
not just meatless meals but mouthwatering menus made up of exciting ingredients filled with glorious flavours to bring
their sunshine to your table even on the
greyest of winter days. Happy cooking!

Breads and Basics

As a food writer, I am constantly trying out and testing new recipes for breads and pastries, dressings and basic sauces. In the end, however, when I want a quick loaf, foolproof pastry or a perfect mayonnaise I can make in seconds, I always return time and time again to a handful of basic recipes.

This section contains these favourites – tried and true old friends that never fail and are versatile enough to be adapted into more elaborate recipes without fear.

Also included in this section are three quick and easy pâtés, which are great standbys to have in the fridge for all sorts of occasions, and three dips which can be made in minutes and may also be used as sauces or dressings.

HOME-MADE BREAD

Makes 1 large loaf

675 g/ 1½ lb STRONG WHITE FLOUR
  (FOR A WHITE LOAF) OR 350 g/
  12 oz STRONG WHITE FLOUR WITH
  350 g/ 12 oz WHOLEMEAL FLOUR
  (FOR A BROWN LOAF)
1 SACHET (1 tbsp) 'EASY-BLEND'
  YEAST
1½ tsp SALT
15 g/ ½ oz BUTTER OR WHITE FAT
450 ml/ ¾ pt HAND-HOT WATER

Place the flour or flours in a large bowl
with the yeast and salt and rub in the
butter or fat as you would for making
pastry, until the mixture resembles
crumbs.

Stir in the hot water and bring the
mixture together to form a ball of dough.

Place the ball of dough on a floured
surface and, holding the ball of dough at
one side with one hand, stretch it away
from you with the heel of the other hand,
using a sort of bashing and pushing
movement. Continue to knead the dough
in this way for a good 10 minutes. Then
fold the dough in half, give the folded
pile a quarter turn on the work surface
and repeat the process.

Form the kneaded dough into an even
ball and place this on a floured board.
Sprinkle the top with flour and cover it
with floured film or a floured light-weight
cloth and leave to rise in a warm place
(not too warm – just an average kitchen
temperature will do!), until doubled in
size. It is better to leave the dough to
rise slowly rather than to force it in an
airing cupboard, for instance. Do make
sure the dough is not in a draught. I find
it also usually takes rather longer for the
dough to rise than it indicates on the
yeast packet. The actual time will
depend on temperature, humidity etc.
Allow 2–3 hours.

Towards the end of this time, preheat
the oven to 230C/450F/gas8. Place a
metal baking tray on a centre shelf and a
small heatproof bowl of boiling water on
the floor of the oven to provide humidity.

When the oven is really hot and the
dough is fully risen, sprinkle the dough
with a little more flour and make two
quick slashes across the top to form a
cross which will help release any uneven
tensions in the dough as it cooks and
produce a nice evenly shaped loaf. It
also gives the bread a home-made look.

With a quick flicking motion, tip the
loaf on the hot baking sheet in the oven,
close the door and bake for 15 minutes.
Then turn down the oven temperature to
190C/375F/gas5 and leave to bake for
30 minutes more. When properly
cooked, the loaf will have a nice brown
crust and should sound 'hollow' when
tapped on the bottom.

'TRENDY' LITTLE BREAD ROLLS

Makes 48

It is a pleasant fashion in trendy restaurants to serve a variety of very small bread rolls in different flavours. These are very easy to produce yourself from the basic bread dough as above.

Begin by dividing the basic quantity of dough in half and trying two of the types of flavouring suggested below. Later you can go on to create your own flavours – the variations are endless.

The flavouring ingredients are mixed in after the dough has been kneaded for 10 minutes. When you begin to mix in the flavourings, especially the oily ones like the olives and the sun-dried tomatoes, it will at first seem difficult – if not impossible. If you persevere, however, after a couple of minutes of kneading the dough will 'accommodate' its flavouring.

Once you have kneaded in the extra flavouring ingredients to each half quantity of basic dough, divide each into 24 even portions. Roll these into round balls and dip the tops first in water and then in a topping, if using one.

Arrange the rolls on greased baking trays (when making a quantity of rolls it is not possible to tip them on a hot baking sheet as I suggest with the large loaf), leaving enough room between each roll for the dough to swell. Cover with floured film or cloth and leave them to rise until they have doubled in size.

Bake the rolls in an oven preheated to 220C/425F/gas7 for 10–15 minutes, until risen and golden.

For the photograph we made four different kinds of roll. Some we simply left plain and others we dipped briefly in cold water and then in sesame seeds or porridge oats, before leaving them to rise.

Flavourings and toppings:
1 To one half quantity of basic dough made with all white flour, mix in about 55 g/2 oz chopped walnuts.

Top half of these with porridge oats.
2 To one half quantity of basic dough made with all white flour, mix in 45 g/ 1½ oz drained and chopped sun-dried tomatoes in oil (available from good delicatessens), 2 teaspoons of concentrated tomato paste and ½ teaspoon dried oregano.
3 To one half quantity of basic dough made with equal parts white and wholemeal flour, mix in 1 crushed garlic clove and 2 tablespoons of finely chopped parsley.
4 To one half quantity of basic dough made with equal parts white and wholemeal flour, mix in 55 g/2 oz stoned and finely chopped olives.

Top half of these with sesame seeds.

WALNUT SODA BREAD

This tasty variation on Irish soda bread uses milk and yogurt instead of the traditional buttermilk, and also includes added walnuts for extra crunch and flavour. The best thing about this bread, however, is that it takes only minutes to prepare.

Makes 1 large loaf

350 g/ 12 oz WHOLEMEAL FLOUR
350 g/ 12 oz STRONG WHITE FLOUR
½ tsp SALT
1 tbsp BICARBONATE OF SODA
2 tbsp CREAM OF TARTAR
2 tsp SUGAR
115 g/ 4 oz SHELLED WALNUTS, COARSELY CHOPPED
250 ml/ 8 fl oz LOW-FAT NATURAL YOGURT
350 ml/ 12 fl oz MILK
VEGETABLE OIL, FOR GREASING

Preheat the oven to 220C/425F/gas7 and grease a baking tray with oil.

In a large bowl, combine the dry ingredients. In another bowl, mix the yogurt with the milk and whisk them until well combined. Then stir this into the dry ingredients and mix well with a fork.

Tip the mixture (which will be fairly soft and moist) out on a floured work surface and, using well-floured hands, bring it together into a ball.

Place this on the prepared baking tray and pat it out to a circle about 3 cm/ 1¼ in thick. Cut the circle into quarters and push these apart a little so there is a thin gap (the width of a pencil) between them. Dust the top with flour and bake immediately for 30 minutes.

This bread is best eaten the same day.

CORN BREAD

There are lots of recipes for different versions of corn bread in the USA. This is my version, which probably isn't authentic but is quite delicious and only takes a few minutes to make.

Corn meal is available from good supermarkets, ethnic grocers and health-food shops. You can also use 'easy-cook' polenta, which is readily available from delicatessens and is pretty much the same thing.

Makes 1 loaf

55 g/ 2 oz BUTTER, MELTED
250 ml/ 8 fl oz LOW-FAT NATURAL YOGURT
125 ml/ 4 fl oz MILK
2 EGGS, BEATEN
115 g/ 4 oz CORN MEAL (SEE ABOVE)
55 g/ 2 oz PLAIN WHITE FLOUR
1 tsp SALT
30 g/ 1 oz SUGAR
1 tbsp BAKING POWDER
GOOD PINCH OF BICARBONATE OF SODA

Banana Bread

Preheat the oven to 200C/400F/gas6 and grease a 1.5 litre/2½ pt loaf tin with a little of the butter.

Mix all the liquid ingredients in one large bowl and all the dry ones in another.

Quickly, and using as few strokes of a spoon as possible, fold the wet ingredients into the dry.

Pour this mixture into the prepared tin and bake for 35 minutes, or until a skewer comes out dry when pushed into the middle of the loaf.

Allow to cool and then slice.

BANANA BREAD

Makes 1 loaf
**115 g/ 4 oz BUTTER, PLUS MORE
   FOR GREASING**
350 g/ 12 oz SELF-RAISING FLOUR
½ tsp SALT
1 tsp CINNAMON
170 g/ 6 oz SOFT BROWN SUGAR
3 EGGS, BEATEN
**3 LARGE BANANAS (ABOUT 450 g/
   1 lb IN TOTAL), PEELED AND
   MASHED OR PURÉED IN A
   BLENDER OR FOOD PROCESSOR**

Preheat the oven to 190C/375F/gas5. Grease a 675 g/1½ lb loaf tin with butter and line the base with greaseproof paper.

Put the flour, salt and cinnamon in a large bowl and mix well.

Put the sugar in another large bowl. Then melt the butter, not allowing it to get too hot, pour it over the sugar and mix well.

Beat the eggs into this gradually. Then add the flour mixture, followed by the bananas and mix well.

Pour this mixture into the prepared tin and bake for 50–60 minutes, or until a skewer inserted into the middle of the loaf comes out clean.

Leave in the tin for 10 minutes, then turn out and allow to cool completely.

CHRISTINE'S SCONES

I thought my scones were pretty good, but my 'big' sister (who always knows better) took me in hand and taught me how to make them the way she learnt at college (many years ago, when scones were scones!).

The scones that follow are, I think – thanks to Christine – not far from perfection! Best made freshly when you need them (which is not a problem as they only take a couple of minutes to make), they do, however, freeze very well.

The first secret to making superior scones is not to have the mixture too dry, the second secret is to make them quickly and handle them as little as possible and the third secret is not to over-cook them.

Makes 8
**55 g/ 2 oz BUTTER, CUT INTO
   SMALL PIECES, PLUS MORE
   FOR GREASING**
225 g/ 8 oz SELF-RAISING FLOUR
GOOD PINCH OF BAKING POWDER
**PINCH OF SALT (MY ADDITION,
   THOUGH NOT STRICTLY
   TRADITIONAL)**
1 tbsp SUGAR
150 ml/ ¼ pt MILK

Preheat the oven to 230C/450F/gas8 and lightly grease a baking tray with some butter.

Sieve the flour into a bowl and add the baking powder, salt and the sugar. Then rub in the butter, as if making pastry, until the mixture resembles fine breadcrumbs.

With a fork, quickly mix in the milk to form a rather soft dough. (This can all be done in seconds in a food processor.)

Tip the dough out on a lightly floured work surface and quickly draw it together to form a ball. Flouring the hands well as the dough will be very soft, quickly pat the dough out to a thickness of about 1 cm/½ in.

Using a 6 cm/2½ in pastry cutter, stamp out 6 rounds. Quickly draw together the remaining dough, pat it out again and cut out 2 more rounds.

Arrange the rounds of dough on the prepared baking tray and bake for 8–10 minutes, until risen and golden.

SHORTCRUST PASTRY

There are so many different kinds of pastry, but time and time again I return to this recipe which works perfectly for most sweet and savoury dishes. It is quick to make, easy to roll out and behaves very well when cooked, being light and crisp but not too fragile.

I have given the traditional method for making it by hand here, but I always make my pastry in a food processor as it takes only seconds.

Makes about 400 g/ 14 oz
225 g/ 8 oz FLOUR
¾ tsp SALT
115 g/ 4 oz COLD BUTTER, CUT INTO
   SMALL PIECES
1 EGG YOLK, LIGHTLY BEATEN

Put the flour and salt in a mixing bowl and rub in the butter until the mixture resembles fine breadcrumbs.

Mix in the egg yolk and 3 tablespoons of cold water. Working quickly, bring the mixture together until it forms a smooth dough.

Wrap in plastic film and chill for 30 minutes before use.

LIGHT VEGETABLE STOCK

Stock may be made from any kind of vegetables, and it is a good idea to make some when you have a surplus.

There are, however, many good vegetable stock cubes available on the market. 'Just Bouillon' are particularly good, contain no artificial additives and come in a variety of flavours. 'Swiss Bouillon Powder', which is available in cardboard drums from health-food shops, is also excellent and very quick and handy to use.

The quantities and ingredients given here are just a guide which you can adapt to whatever ingredients you have to hand. The onion skins will give your finished stock a lovely golden glow.

Makes about 1.75 litres/ 3 pt
115 g/ 4 oz MUSHROOMS, SLICED
450 g/ 1 lb ONIONS, QUARTERED,
   BUT SKINS LEFT ON (SEE ABOVE)
225 g/ 8 oz CARROTS, COARSELY CHOPPED
225 g/ 8 oz SWEDE, PARSNIP OR
   TURNIP, COARSELY CHOPPED
3 GARLIC CLOVES
STRIP OF THINLY PARED RIND
   FROM AN UNWAXED LEMON,
   ABOUT 5 cm/ 2 in LONG
LARGE BUNCH OF PARSLEY
   (COMPLETE WITH STALKS)
SMALL BUNCH OF OTHER HERBS
   AS AVAILABLE
1 BAY LEAF
2 tsp SALT
1 tsp SUGAR
SALT AND PEPPER
GOOD DASH OF SOY SAUCE

Put all the ingredients in a large pan with 2 litres/3½ pt of water and some salt and pepper.

Bring to the boil and then simmer gently for 1½ hours.

Strain and discard the solids.

VINAIGRETTE

This is a basic recipe which can be varied according to taste or to suit the ingredients of the salad it is to dress.

Try different oils, like walnut or hazelnut, or a mixture. Experiment with flavoured vinegars or substitute lemon or lime juice. 'Spike' your dressing with a little horseradish, crushed garlic or chilli instead of mustard or add small quantities of chopped herbs.

Makes about 4 tbsp
1 tbsp WHITE WINE VINEGAR
¼ tsp SALT
GOOD TWIST OF FRESHLY GROUND
   BLACK PEPPER
½ tsp SUGAR
¼ tsp ENGLISH MUSTARD POWDER
3 tbsp EXTRA VIRGIN OLIVE OIL

Place the vinegar, salt and pepper, sugar and mustard in a screw-top jar, seal and shake until the sugar has dissolved.

Add the oil and shake again until amalgamated. If possible, leave for 30 minutes to an hour before using to allow the flavours to develop.

Shake well again before use.

MAYONNAISE

All the worries of making home-made mayonnaise are taken away by using a food processor or liquidizer. It never fails and takes no more time to make from scratch than it does to open a jar.

The flavour will depend on the oil you use. A strong fruity extra virgin olive oil will naturally produce a strong fruity flavoured mayonnaise, especially good if converted into aïoli with the addition of crushed garlic. If you want a milder flavour, use a milder-flavoured oil or half olive oil and half flavourless vegetable oil.

Makes about 250 ml/ 8 fl oz
1 EGG (AT ROOM TEMPERATURE)
1 tsp SALT
½ tsp ENGLISH MUSTARD POWDER
175 ml/ 6 fl oz OLIVE OIL
   (SEE ABOVE)
PEPPER (WHITE IS PREFERABLE TO
   BLACK, WHICH PRODUCES LITTLE
   DARK SPECKS)
GOOD SQUEEZE OF LEMON JUICE

Put the egg, salt and mustard in the bowl of a food processor or liquidizer and blend until smooth.

With the motor still running, add the oil in a thin steady trickle. You can pour a little quicker as the mayonnaise starts to thicken.

Add pepper and lemon juice to taste. If the mayonnaise is too thick, add 1–2 tablespoons of boiling water and blend briefly.

Mayonnaise in the gravy boat and Vinaigrette in the glass jug, together with an assortment of flavoured oils and vinegars.

HOLLANDAISE SAUCE

One of the richest and most luxurious of all the classic French sauces, hollandaise is best reserved for special occasions – perhaps as a reward after a week of particularly healthy low-fat eating! It transforms any plainly cooked vegetable into a treat, and is really sublime with asparagus.

It is a notoriously tricky sauce to make. With the help of a blender or food processor, however, this 'cheat's' version is child's play.

Makes about 150 ml/ ¼ pt
2 EGG YOLKS
1 tbsp LEMON JUICE
85 g/ 3 oz UNSALTED BUTTER
SALT AND PEPPER

Put the egg yolks, lemon juice and 1 teaspoon of water in the bowl of a blender or food processor and whizz until well blended and frothy.

Meanwhile, melt the butter in a small saucepan and heat until bubbling – but do not allow it to brown.

With the motor of the processor or liquidizer still running, add the melted butter in a slow steady stream and continue to process for a few seconds longer. Season to taste.

Transfer the mixture to a double boiler or a bowl set over a pan of very gently simmering water. Stir constantly until thickened.

If you do not want to use the sauce immediately, keep it warm for up to 15 minutes simply by removing the pan from the stove and leaving the bowl sitting over the warm water. However, keep stirring occasionally for another minute or so, as it will continue to cook for a little while after you remove it from the heat.

CUMBERLAND SAUCE

This lovely simple old-fashioned fruity sauce is traditionally associated with meat and meat pies, but is also perfect with all kinds of meatless dishes like the Chestnut, Apple and Onion Pie in the Christmas menu starting on page 26.

The sauce may be served hot or cold, but I prefer it cold.

Makes about 300 ml/ ½ pt
1 UNWAXED LEMON
1 UNWAXED ORANGE
¼ tsp ENGLISH MUSTARD POWDER
6 DROPS OF TABASCO SAUCE OR A
　GOOD PINCH OF CAYENNE PEPPER
PINCH OF SALT
100 ml/ 3½ fl oz PORT
115 g/ 4 oz REDCURRANT JELLY

Thinly peel the rind from half the lemon and half the orange and cut this rind into the thinnest possible 'needles'. Blanch them in a small pan of boiling water for 5 minutes. Drain them, refresh in cold water and drain again.

Squeeze the juice from the lemon and orange into a small pan. Mix in the mustard, Tabasco or cayenne and salt and stir until dissolved. Add the port and the redcurrant jelly, bring to the boil and simmer for 5 minutes, or until the jelly has completely dissolved.

Strain the sauce through a sieve into a jug or serving dish and stir in the 'needles' of blanched citrus rind. Reheat if serving hot, or chill if serving cold.

Cumberland Sauce

Put the shallots, wine and vinegar in a small pan and simmer over a low heat until reduced to about 2 tablespoons (this takes about 5 minutes, and must be done slowly to cook the shallot and allow it to give off its flavour).

Over a low to moderate heat, whisk in the chilled butter, two pieces at a time (as soon each pair have melted, add two more). It should take 3–4 minutes to incorporate all the butter. If at any time the sauce begins to bubble, remove the pan from the heat for a moment as the butter will become oily if it gets too hot. The finished sauce should be pale, creamy and emulsified. Season to taste with salt and pepper.

The sauce should be served warm but can be kept hot over a pan of hot water for about 15 minutes.

HUMMUS

This popular Middle-Eastern dip, made from chickpeas and tahini is now available in most delicatessens and supermarkets. With the aid of a blender or food processor, however, it takes seconds to make at home and is, of course, much cheaper.

Tahini is a paste made from sesame seeds and is available from health-food shops and large supermarkets. You can make tahini at home in a blender or food processor, but don't over-process as the finished purée should have some texture.

Makes about 300 ml/ ½ pt
400 g/ 14 oz CANNED CHICKPEAS,
   DRAINED AND RINSED
1 GARLIC CLOVE, CRUSHED
4 tbsp TAHINI
JUICE OF ½ LEMON
SALT
To garnish
1 tbsp OLIVE OIL
GOOD PINCH OF PAPRIKA
1 tsp FINELY CHOPPED PARSLEY

BEURRE BLANC

Some cooks strain off the shallots once they have given off their flavour, but I prefer to leave them in the finished sauce.

This sauce is perfect with all vegetables and many savoury dishes.

Makes about 300 ml/ ½ pt
2 SHALLOTS, FINELY CHOPPED
3 tbsp WHITE WINE
3 tbsp WHITE WINE VINEGAR
225 g/ 8 oz CHILLED UNSALTED
   BUTTER, CUT INTO
   2.5 cm/ 1 in CUBES
SALT AND PEPPER

Put the chickpeas, garlic, tahini and lemon juice in the bowl of a blender or food processor and blend until smooth. Season to taste with salt.

Spoon the mixture into a serving dish and smooth with the back of a spoon. Drizzle over the olive oil and sprinkle over the paprika and chopped parsley

GUACAMOLE

This delicious invention from Central America is based on the versatile avocado, and can be used as a dip for crudités, corn chips and other biscuits (try the Corn Wafers on page 82), or as a sauce for cooked foods.

This is one time I don't use my food processor, as it would make the texture too smooth. You can leave out the chilli if you like – or add more!

Makes about 250 ml/ 8 fl oz
1 LARGE, OR 1½ SMALL, VERY RIPE
   AVOCADO(S)
115 g/ 4 oz CHOPPED RIPE
   TOMATOES
1 GARLIC CLOVE, CRUSHED
2 SPRING ONIONS, FINELY
   CHOPPED
1–2 CHILLI PEPPERS, DESEEDED
   AND FINELY CHOPPED (OPTIONAL)
JUICE OF 1 LIME OR LEMON
1 tbsp CHOPPED CORIANDER
   LEAVES
SALT AND PEPPER
LIME WEDGES AND CORIANDER
   SPRIGS, TO GARNISH (OPTIONAL)

Peel and stone the avocado(s) and then roughly mash the flesh with a fork.

Immediately mix this together with all the remaining ingredients and season to taste with salt and pepper.

Spoon into a serving dish and garnish with lime wedges and coriander sprigs, if using.

LENTIL AND SUN-DRIED TOMATO PÂTÉ

This tasty pâté couldn't be easier to make and yet is full of deceptively complex flavours. It is best served with hot toast.

The kind of stock you use will subtly change the flavour – I like to use an onion-based stock cube for this recipe.

Sun-dried tomatoes preserved in oil are available from delicatessens.

Makes about 450 g/ 1 lb
225 g/ 8 oz RED LENTILS
700 ml/ 1¼ pt VEGETABLE STOCK
   (SEE ABOVE)
55 g/ 2 oz SUN-DRIED TOMATOES
   IN OIL, DRAINED
SALT AND PEPPER
FRESH TOMATO WEDGES AND
   SPRIGS OF BASIL, TO
   GARNISH (OPTIONAL)

Put the lentils and stock in a small saucepan and bring slowly to the boil.

Cover and simmer over as low a heat as possible, undisturbed, until almost all the stock has been absorbed. (This will take about 15–20 minutes. Watch towards the end to make sure the pan doesn't burn.) Remove the lid for the last couple of minutes of cooking time to allow any remaining moisture to evaporate.

Allow the lentils to cool, then tip them into the bowl of a blender or food processor. Add the sun-dried tomatoes and process until smooth. Season to taste with salt and pepper.

Spoon the mixture into a serving dish and garnish with tomato wedges and sprigs of basil, if using.

CLOCKWISE FROM THE BOTTOM LEFT: *Scorched Pepper, Walnut and Ricotta Pâté (page 24), Corn Wafers (page 82), Lentil and Sun-dried Tomato Pâté, and Mushroom Pâté (page 24).*

AUBERGINE AND SESAME DIP

This smoky-tasting paste can be used as dip, as a spread or as a filling for pastry cases or stuffed vegetables. Thinned with a little vegetable stock, it may also be used as a pouring sauce for cooked dishes.

Makes about 250 ml/ 8 fl oz

2 AUBERGINES (TOTAL WEIGHT
   ABOUT 450 g/ 1 lb)
1 SMALL MILD ONION, VERY
   FINELY CHOPPED
2 GARLIC CLOVES, CRUSHED
1 heaped tbsp TAHINI (SEE RECIPE FOR HUMMUS
   ON PAGE 21)
GOOD PINCH OF CHILLI POWDER
4 tbsp CHOPPED CORIANDER
SALT AND PEPPER
1 tbsp EXTRA VIRGIN OLIVE OIL,
   TO DRESS

Preheat the oven to 200C/400F/gas6 and then bake the aubergines whole for about 15 minutes, or until quite soft.

Allow them to cool and then scoop out all the flesh and discard the skins.

Mash the flesh well and mix thoroughly with all the other ingredients except 1 tablespoon of the coriander.

Spoon this mixture into a serving dish, smooth with the back of the spoon and then drizzle over the olive oil and garnish with the reserved coriander.

SCORCHED PEPPER, WALNUT AND RICOTTA PÂTÉ

The subtle taste of this creamy pâté contrasts the sweet smoky flavours of the grilled pepper with the earthy taste of walnuts – plus a little added 'bite' of horseradish.

Ricotta is a mild-tasting Italian fresh cheese and is available from delicatessens and large supermarkets.

Makes about 450 g/ 1 lb

1 tbsp WALNUT OR OLIVE OIL
2 RED SWEET PEPPERS,
   QUARTERED LENGTHWISE
   AND DESEEDED
170 g/ 6 oz RICOTTA CHEESE
85 g/ 3 oz SHELLED WALNUTS,
   FINELY CHOPPED
1 tbsp HORSERADISH SAUCE
JUICE OF ½ LEMON
SALT AND PEPPER
VEGETABLE OIL, FOR GREASING

Preheat a hot grill and line the grill pan with foil. Lightly grease the foil with oil.

Arrange the quartered peppers, skin side up, in one layer in the prepared grill pan and grill them until all the skin is blackened.

Put the pepper quarters in a plastic bag and allow them to cook in their own steam for 5 minutes. Then remove the blackened skins over a bowl to catch any juices.

Put the peppers and any juices in the bowl of a blender or food processor together with the other ingredients and seasoning to taste. Process until smooth.

Transfer the mixture to a serving bowl or plate and chill for at least 1 hour to allow the flavours to develop fully.

Scorched Pepper, Walnut and Ricotta Pâté served with Corn Wafers (page 82)

MUSHROOM PÂTÉ

This succulent pâté will be a huge success with all mushroom lovers. In fact, it has so much flavour that you might have to convince dedicated vegetarians that they aren't actually eating meat. Add a few soaked dried wild mushrooms for an even fuller flavour – and, for very special occasions, garnish with truffles instead of mushrooms!

Serve with hot toast and pickled gherkins or, even better, pickled walnuts.

To clarify butter, simply melt it in a small pan over a low heat and then pour it off gently, leaving the unwanted sediment behind in the pan.

Makes about 450 g/ 1 lb

1 tbsp EXTRA VIRGIN OLIVE OIL
1 ONION, FINELY CHOPPED
225 g/ 8 oz MUSHROOMS, FINELY
   CHOPPED (OPEN ONES WILL HAVE
   MORE FLAVOUR)
1 GARLIC CLOVE, CRUSHED
2 tbsp FINELY CHOPPED PARSLEY
375 g/ 13 oz CANNED CANNELLINI
   BEANS, DRAINED AND RINSED
SALT AND PEPPER
To garnish
1 BAY LEAF
FEW SMALL THIN SLICES OF
   BUTTON MUSHROOM
2 tbsp CLARIFIED BUTTER
   (SEE ABOVE)

Heat the oil in a small, preferably non-stick, pan and cook the onion over a moderate heat for about 5 minutes, or until soft and translucent.

Add the mushrooms, garlic and parsley and continue to cook, stirring occasionally, for about 10 minutes more, until they have softened and the liquid which comes out of the mushrooms has evaporated. Season well with salt and pepper.

Tip the contents of the pan into the bowl of a blender or food processor. Add the drained beans and process to a very smooth purée.

Pack this into an attractive small dish or terrine and make the top as flat and smooth as possible. Garnish by placing the bay leaf in the middle and arrange the mushroom slices around it attractively.

Gently pour over the clarified butter, being careful not to dislodge the garnish, and chill for at least 4 hours, or overnight, to allow the flavours to develop.

The Menus

For a meal to be a complete
success it must consist of a well-
balanced selection of dishes. In a
carnivore's diet, tradition makes
this relatively easy for the cook
to plan. When designing a
vegetarian meal, however, a
little more thought is needed to
achieve the perfect balance
between flavours, textures and
colours.

I have therefore done part of the
work for you by grouping the
dishes in this book into carefully
thought-out menus each to serve
6 people.

Of course, not all of us like the
same things. You might hate
soup, for instance, or prefer one
of your own puddings. The
menus are meant only as
guidelines, so do adapt them
as you would season the
recipes — to taste.

Happy cooking!

Festive Feasting

This sophisticated winter menu includes many familiar festive flavours and is designed for Christmas lunch or dinner, or any other special occasion in the holiday season which calls for an elegant meatless meal.

SALAD OF RED AND GREEN LEAVES WITH FETA, WALNUTS AND MOSTARDA FRUITS

CHESTNUT, APPLE AND ONION PIE CUMBERLAND SAUCE HUNGARIAN BRAISED RED CABBAGE CHOPSTICK POTATOES

CHRISTMAS PUDDING ICE-CREAM

SALAD OF RED AND GREEN LEAVES WITH FETA, WALNUTS AND MOSTARDA FRUITS

This is my favourite salad of the moment and is good at any time of the year, but somehow it fits the bill perfectly as a festive starter, particularly at Christmas with its combination of red and green leaves and the glistening jewel-like mostarda fruits looking like decorations on the tree.

Mostarda fruits are an unusual and delicious Italian preserve made from crystallized fruits in a heavy mustard-flavoured syrup. Traditionally eaten in Italy with hot and cold meats of all kinds, they are incredibly versatile and have many uses for non-meat-eaters too! They are available in jars from good delicatessens. As is balsamic vinegar, which is made in Modena from grape juice concentrate and aged for 15–20 years in wooden casks to give it a dark sweet-and-sour taste.

400 g/ 14 oz ITALIAN
MOSTARDA FRUITS (SEE ABOVE)
225 g/ 8 oz MIXED RED AND
GREEN LEAVES
3 tbsp OLIVE OIL
2 GARLIC CLOVES, THINLY SLICED
85 g/ 3 oz WHITE BREAD, CUT INTO
1 cm/ ¹/₂ in CUBES
115 g/ 4 oz SHELLED WALNUTS
170 g/ 6 oz FETA CHEESE, CUT INTO
1 cm/ ¹/₂ in CUBES
For the dressing
1 tbsp BALSAMIC VINEGAR
3 tbsp EXTRA VIRGIN OLIVE OIL
SALT AND PEPPER

Drain the mostarda fruits, reserving 1 tablespoon of the syrup. Remove any stones and roughly chop the fruits.

Arrange the leaves decoratively on 6 large plates.

In a wok or frying pan, heat the oil over a low to moderate heat and gently stir-fry the garlic and bread cubes until the bread is golden and crispy. Discard the garlic and drain the croutons on kitchen paper.

Make the dressing: place all the ingredients in a small screw-top jar together with the reserved syrup. Seal and shake until well amalgamated.

Sprinkle the croutons, walnut pieces, cheese and mostarda fruits over the leaves. Drizzle the salad with the dressing and serve immediately.

CHESTNUT, APPLE AND ONION PIE

This unusual pie is loosely based on a traditional recipe from the gloriously wild hills of the Cévennes in southern France. There chestnuts were once the main crop and were relied on as a staple by the poor country folk, who thought up every imaginable way of using them in both sweet and savoury dishes. The original recipe contained some pork, but this version is just as tasty.

Cooking and peeling chestnuts is, I am afraid, a bore. They are best roasted, otherwise boil them. If you simply can't face the effort, use canned whole chestnuts. Alternatively, some shops sell really good ones in vacuum packs. The making of the rest of the pie is simplicity itself.

550 g/ 1¹/₄ lb SHORTCRUST PASTRY
(SEE PAGE 18)
For the filling
2 tbsp OLIVE OIL
350 g/ 12 oz ONION, CHOPPED
450 g/ 1 lb EATING APPLES (COX'S IF
POSSIBLE), PEELED AND CORED
285–325 g/ 10–11 oz COOKED PEELED
CHESTNUTS (SEE ABOVE)
1 tsp CHOPPED FRESH THYME OR
¹/₂ tsp DRIED
1 tsp CHOPPED FRESH SAGE OR
¹/₂ tsp DRIED
3 EGGS
SALT AND PEPPER
MILK, FOR GLAZING

Preheat the oven to 200C/400F/gas6.

Heat the oil in a sauté pan over a moderate heat and cook the onion until golden brown.

Meanwhile chop the apples into small pieces (about 6 mm/¹/₄ in). Don't use the food processor, or you might end up with a mush. Tip these into a large bowl and add the onions.

Cut the chestnuts into quarters and add them to the bowl together with the herbs. Season well and mix thoroughly.

Beat two of the eggs, add these to the bowl and mix in well.

Roll out two-thirds of the pastry and use it to line the bottom of a non-stick loose-bottomed fluted 24 cm/9¹/₂ in flan tin. Fill with the chestnut mixture, smoothing it into a nice mound shape.

Roll out the rest of the pastry to make a lid. Place on top of the pie, sealing the edges with a little water. Decorate the top of the pie with pastry trimmings.

Beat the remaining egg with a little milk and use some of this to glaze the pie.

Bake for 40–50 minutes or until golden brown. If you like, 10 minutes before the pie is cooked, carefully remove the sides of the tin, brush the sides of the pie with the remaining egg glaze and return to the oven to brown the sides.

Serve hot with Cumberland Sauce (see page 20).

HUNGARIAN BRAISED RED CABBAGE

The original Hungarian recipe for this succulent fragrant dish uses goose fat or lard, but this version uses olive oil and tastes even better.

1 tbsp OLIVE OIL
1 ONION, CHOPPED
900 g/ 2 lb RED CABBAGE,
   FINELY SHREDDED
450 g/ 1 lb WHITE CABBAGE, FINELY
   SHREDDED
3 tbsp WHITE WINE VINEGAR OR
   CIDER VINEGAR
2 tbsp SUGAR
1 BAY LEAF
SALT AND PEPPER
450 ml/ ¾ pt VEGETABLE STOCK

In a large saucepan which has a lid, heat the oil over a moderate heat and cook the onion in it until golden.

Add all the remaining ingredients and mix well.

Bring to the boil. Cover and simmer for about 30 minutes, or until the cabbage is tender.

CHOPSTICK POTATOES

These are really simply a variation of classic roast potatoes, which need not be taboo to vegetarians just because they are traditionally cooked around a roast, or in meat fat in a separate pan. Roast potatoes cooked in olive oil are even tastier, and this 'chopstick' slicing method not only makes for an unusual and attractive presentation, but means that the potatoes end up with more crispy outside bits! If you are cooking them in the oven with the pie, they will need to go in 10–15 minutes before it does.

3 tbsp EXTRA VIRGIN OLIVE OIL
9 EVENLY SHAPED MEDIUM-SIZED
   OLD POTATOES (ABOUT 1.35 K/
   3 lb IN TOTAL)
COARSE SEA SALT
PEPPER

Preheat the oven to 200C/400F/ gas6 and grease a baking tin with 1 tablespoon of the oil.

Peel the potatoes and cut them in half lengthwise. Cook in boiling salted water for 5 minutes and then drain.

Place each potato half, cut side down, on a chopping board and place a chopstick running lengthwise on either side of it.

Using a sharp knife, make vertical cuts across the potato about 6 mm/¼ in apart. (The chopsticks will prevent the knife from cutting right through the potato.)

Arrange the potato 'chopsticks' in the prepared baking tin. Drizzle the remaining oil over the potatoes, allowing it seep into the slits.

Roast for about 1 hour (see above), or until crisp and golden. Baste the potatoes a couple of times during the process, sprinkling them with sea salt and pepper about 15 minutes before the end of cooking.

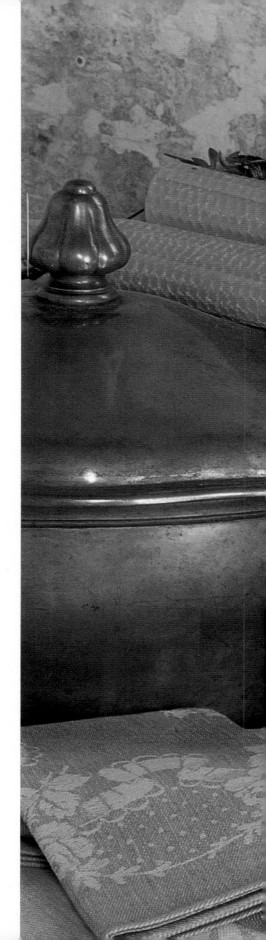

CHRISTMAS PUDDING ICE-CREAM

This is a wonderfully simple idea from Australia, where they celebrate Christmas in the middle of summer. It makes a pleasant change from the, somewhat heavier, traditional pudding with brandy butter – although it is still hardly food for weight-watchers!

Vegetarians must be careful when buying ready-made Christmas puddings, as many contain beef suet. Read the ingredients label carefully. The easiest solution, however, is to make your own from a classic recipe and substitute vegetarian suet, which is available from all supermarkets.

500 ml/ 16 fl oz BEST-QUALITY READY-MADE VANILLA ICE-CREAM
225 g/ 8 oz CHRISTMAS PUDDING (SEE ABOVE), MASHED OR CRUMBLED FINELY

First allow the ice-cream to soften slightly by removing it from the freezer for 10–15 minutes.

Tip the softened ice-cream into a bowl and quickly but thoroughly mix in the crumbled Christmas pudding.

Return the mixture to the freezer to firm it up.

Party Finger-food

Bite-sized and beautiful, this collection of delicious nibbles makes a perfect drinks party menu for any time of the year. Allow 6–8 'bites' per guest.

DEEP-FRIED CAMEMBERT-STUFFED OLIVES

STUFFED VINE LEAVES

MINI 'PIZZAS'

CRUDITÉS WITH DIPS

BÖREKS WITH SPINACH AND RICOTTA

TEENY-WEENY 'BLINIS'

DEEP-FRIED CAMEMBERT-STUFFED OLIVES

These are much easier to make than they sound and are absolutely delicious, so do try them. However, if you can't get anyone else to do the last-minute frying for you, don't forget to put on a pinny over your best frock – not only to guard it from splashed fat, but to ensure that you don't rejoin your guests smelling like a chip shop!

If you don't own a cherry/olive stoner, invest in one – or don't even attempt this recipe!

Makes 24

24 OF THE BIGGEST BLACK OLIVES
YOU CAN FIND
55 g/ 2 oz CAMEMBERT CHEESE
1 EGG, BEATEN
4 tbsp FINE BREADCRUMBS
FLOUR, FOR DUSTING
VEGETABLE OIL, FOR DEEP-FRYING

Stone the olives and stuff the resulting cavity with a little piece of the Camembert cheese.

Put the flour, beaten egg and breadcrumbs in three separate bowls.

Dip the stuffed olives first in the flour, then in the beaten egg, and then finally in the breadcrumbs.

Heat the oil until just smoking and deep-fry the coated olives for a couple of minutes, until golden brown and crisp.

Drain for a few seconds on paper towels, then serve immediately.

STUFFED VINE LEAVES

Versions of these nibbles are served all over Greece, Turkey and the Middle East as part of the pre-meal mezze or snacks.

If you are lucky enough to have fresh vine leaves, boil them for 5 minutes in salted water. Then drain and refresh them in cold water before use. Preserved vine leaves are available in plastic packs or canned from delicatessens or large supermarkets. Prepare them for use according to the package instructions. Either type of leaf should be well dried on tea towels or paper towels.

The stuffed vine leaves are nice served with Greek-style yogurt as a dip.

4 tbsp EXTRA VIRGIN OLIVE OIL
1 LARGE ONION, CHOPPED
115 g/ 4 oz BASMATI RICE, RINSED
AND DRIED
55 g/ 2 oz CURRANTS
55 g/ 2 oz PINE KERNELS
2 tbsp CHOPPED MINT, DILL OR
PARSLEY (IN THAT ORDER OF
PREFERENCE)
250 ml/ 8 fl oz VEGETABLE STOCK
1 tsp SALT
225 g/ 8 oz VINE LEAVES
(SEE ABOVE)
JUICE OF 1 LEMON
PEPPER

Heat half the oil in a small to medium heavy-based saucepan over a moderate heat and cook the onion, stirring occasionally, for about 5 minutes or until soft and translucent.

Add the rice and stir well until each grain is coated with oil. Cover and cook over the lowest possible heat, stirring occasionally, for 5 minutes more.

Add the fruit, nuts, herbs, stock, salt and a couple of good grinds of pepper. Simmer, uncovered, for about 5 minutes or until all the liquid has been absorbed.

Place the vine leaves shiny side down, and put about 1 heaped teaspoon of the rice mixture in the middle of each. Fold over the stem end of each, then fold in the sides and roll it up into a little

parcel. Do not roll them too tightly as the rice will swell when the parcels are cooked. Continue until you have used up all the leaves or all the filling. (The number that you make will depend very much on the size of the leaves.)

Arrange the little parcels, seam-side down, in a large pan which has a lid (I use a sauté pan), in layers if necessary.

Drizzle over the remaining olive oil and the lemon juice. Then add just enough hot water barely to cover the parcels. Place a suitable plate on top of the parcels to stop them jiggling about and coming undone as they cook.

Cover the pan and cook over the lowest possible heat for 1 hour. Check halfway through to make sure that the liquid hasn't all evaporated, adding a little more if necessary.

Remove from the heat and allow the stuffed vine leaves to cool in the liquid. Drain and arrange on a plate.

MINI 'PIZZAS'

These mouthwatering little bites are made not with bread dough, but with bought puff pastry. One 375 g/ 13 oz packet will make about 48. This sounds a lot, but they will disappear in minutes.

Makes 48

Preheat the oven to 220C/425F/gas7.

Simply roll out the pastry as thinly as possible and then stamp out bite-sized circles with a small pastry cutter or the rim of a suitable small glass.

Add the toppings of choice and then bake for about 7–10 minutes.

Suggestions for toppings: try olive paste and pesto (from delicatessens); slivers of Mozzarella, chèvre and other good well-flavoured cheeses; slivers of sun-dried tomatoes (from delicatessens); slices of small black olives, pieces of scorched pepper (see page 24), small chunks of avocado (delicious hot!) – the possibilities are endless.

Preheat the oven to 180C/350F/gas4 and grease a baking tray with a little of the butter.

Heat the oil in a pan over a moderate heat and cook the onion, stirring, for about 5 minutes or until soft and translucent.

Add the spinach and continue to cook, stirring constantly, for another 2–3 minutes, or just until it just begins to wilt. Do not overcook or the spinach will turn to a mush.

Transfer the contents of the pan to a bowl and allow to cool.

In another bowl, mash the cheese with a fork, then mix in the egg and whisk until smooth. Season well with salt and pepper.

Mix in the pine kernels and the spinach mixture. (The filling looks most unprepossessing at this stage but do not worry.)

Lay one sheet of filo pastry (see above) on a work surface with the long edges running away from you and brush it all over with melted butter.

Cut the piece of pastry lengthwise into 4 equal long strips and place a heaped teaspoon of the filling on each of the nearer ends.

Working one strip at a time, fold one edge diagonally over the filling to make a triangle, bringing the corner up to meet the opposite side. Continue folding up the pastry in this manner to make a neat triangular parcel.

As the parcels are made, arrange them seam-side down on the prepared baking tray. Continue until all the pastry and all the filling are used up. Brush the tops of the parcels with the remaining butter and bake for 40–45 minutes, or until crisp and golden. Serve immediately.

CRUDITÉS WITH DIPS

In France I often choose a simple plate of 'crudités' as a first course. However, what arrives on the table will not be the same as the raw unadorned 'crudités' which have become the healthy and popular snack and party food on this side of the Channel. In France they will consist of an assortment of dressed vegetable salads. Oddly enough, moreover, a good proportion of these vegetables might be cooked – not raw – like beetroot or even asparagus in season.

For this menu, however, I suggest serving a selection of raw vegetables, cut into manageable bite-sized (or two-bite-sized) pieces, which are convenient for scooping up a variety of thick dressings or dips. As big a selection as possible looks impressive and attractive.

Choose from: spring onions, celery, sweet peppers, carrots, radishes, broccoli and cauliflower florets, crunchy cabbage strips, mange-tout and snap peas.

When in season, nothing is more delicious raw than fresh peas or young broad beans. So remove them from their shells and either offer them in little bowls to be eaten like peanuts or thread bite-sized rows of them on wooden cocktail sticks to be 'dipped'.

Choose a selection of dips from the Breads and Basics section, beginning on page 21.

BÖREKS WITH SPINACH AND RICOTTA

These mouthwatering little filo pastry parcels are much quicker and easier to make than you might imagine. Once you have learnt the knack of folding the pastry you can experiment with your own fillings.

Filo pastry is available fresh or frozen from delicatessens and supermarkets. It dries out and becomes brittle very quickly so you must only work with one sheet at a time, re-rolling the rest of the sheets each time you remove one, and covering the roll with a plastic film and a slightly damp tea towel.

85 g/ 3 oz MELTED BUTTER

2 tbsp OLIVE OIL

1 SMALL ONION, FINELY CHOPPED

225 g/ 8 oz SPINACH, FINELY CHOPPED AND THOROUGHLY DRIED

85 g/ 3 oz RICOTTA CHEESE

1 EGG

2 tbsp PINE KERNELS

6 SHEETS OF FILO PASTRY (SEE ABOVE), DEFROSTED IF FROZEN

SALT AND PEPPER

TEENY-WEENY 'BLINIS'

Although Russian in inspiration, my versions of these little pancakes are far from authentic as they are leavened with baking powder instead of yeast. This makes them much quicker and easier – and just as nice, I think.

You can top them with whatever you fancy: a dollop of cream cheese, fromage frais or Greek-style yogurt is good garnished with chopped hard-boiled egg, onion, gherkins, capers or other pickles. Alternatively, try any of the pâtés or dips on pages 21–24 in the Breads and Basics section, topped with fresh herbs or other suitable garnishes.

Makes 48

225 g/ 8 oz FLOUR

2 heaped tsp BAKING POWDER

1 tsp SALT

275 ml/ 9 fl oz MILK

2 EGGS, BEATEN

PEPPER

VEGETABLE OIL, FOR FRYING

TOPPINGS OF CHOICE (SEE ABOVE)

In a bowl, mix together the flour, baking powder and salt and season with a few twists of pepper. Add the milk and eggs and beat to form a smooth batter.

Lightly oil a frying pan and place it over a moderate heat. When hot, drop teaspoonfuls of batter into the pan. (about 4 at a time.)

Cook the blinis for 2–3 minutes, turning once, or until cooked through and golden brown on each side.

If you want to serve them hot, keep them warm in a covered dish in a low oven while cooking the remaining batches. However, I generally serve them cold as it is less last-minute bother. Any extras freeze well.

Add toppings of your choice to serve.

Beautiful Breakfasts

Make time occasionally to prepare a really special breakfast, and remember there is life beyond bacon and eggs or croissants and coffee. So invite friends over on Sunday for a lazy convivial morning complete with mouthwatering food and the papers.

PASSION FRUIT MUFFINS WITH PRESERVES

BANANA BREAD FRENCH TOAST WITH DRIED FRUIT COMPOTE

POACHED EGGS ON POTATO CAKES WITH HOLLANDAISE SAUCE

FROMAGE FRAIS WITH MELON PURÉE

PASSION FRUIT MUFFINS WITH PRESERVES

These American-style muffins are best eaten warm straight from the oven. As they take only minutes to prepare, they are ideal for special breakfasts and make a refreshing change from croissants or brioche.

45 g/ 1½ oz MELTED BUTTER, PLUS
    MORE FOR GREASING
255 g/ 9 oz FLOUR, SIFTED
1 heaped tbsp BAKING POWDER
½ tsp SALT
1 tbsp SUGAR
JUICE AND PULP OF 4
    PASSION FRUIT
250 ml/ 8 fl oz MILK
1 EGG, LIGHTLY BEATEN
To serve
BUTTER, FROMAGE FRAIS,
    GREEK-STYLE YOGURT OR THICK
    SOUR CREAM
JAMS OR PRESERVES, OR MORE
    PASSION FRUIT

Preheat the oven to 220C/425F/gas7 and butter a sheet of 12 deep patty moulds (or 2 smaller ones of 6).

Mix the flour, baking powder, salt and sugar in one large bowl and the remaining ingredients in another (or in a measuring jug).

Tip the liquid ingredients into the dry ones and mix them together very quickly just until the flour is moistened – but do not beat the mixture!

Divide this between the prepared patty tins and bake for 20–25 minutes, until well risen and a skewer inserted into the middle of a muffin comes out clean.

Tip them out on a wire rack, allow them to cool for 1–2 minutes and then serve warm. (Any leftover muffins are also nice cold.)

Serve the muffins with butter and jams or preserves, or perhaps a dish of fromage frais, Greek-style yogurt or thick sour cream with the juice and pulp of a couple more passion fruit poured over the top.

BANANA BREAD FRENCH TOAST WITH DRIED FRUIT COMPOTE

This is a wonderfully satisfying fruity breakfast dish. The bread and the compote can be made the day before.

3 EGGS, LIGHTLY BEATEN
6 tbsp MILK
6 SLICES OF BANANA BREAD (SEE
    PAGE 17), ABOUT 1 cm/ ½ in
    THICK
85 g/ 3 oz BUTTER
6 tbsp CRÈME FRAÎCHE OR
    GREEK-STYLE YOGURT, TO
    SERVE (OPTIONAL)
For the compote
225 g/ 8 oz NO-SOAK
    DRIED PRUNES
225 g/ 8 oz NO-SOAK
    DRIED APRICOTS
450 ml/ ¾ pt ORANGE JUICE
    (IF FROM A CARTON, USE THE
    PURE UNSWEETENED KIND)
3 tbsp CHUNKY ORANGE MARMALADE

The day before, make the compote: place all the ingredients in a heavy-based pan which has a tight-fitting lid. Bring to the boil. Turn down the heat, cover and simmer for 30 minutes, stirring occasionally. Allow to cool.

Next day, mix the eggs and milk thoroughly in a shallow dish or soup plate and dip the slices of banana bread in it until thoroughly soaked on both sides.

Melt the butter in a frying pan over a low to moderate heat and cook the slices of bread in it until browned on both sides. Drain for a few seconds on paper towels and cut each slice of bread in half.

While the bread is frying, reheat the compote gently.

Arrange the slices of 'French toast' on 6 warmed plates and top with some of the fruit compote and cream or yogurt, if using.

POACHED EGGS ON POTATO CAKES WITH HOLLANDAISE SAUCE

There are lots of recipes for old-fashioned potato cakes, but this is my own version which is 'spiked' with chopped spring onion.

Many people find poaching eggs very difficult, as the eggs tend to spread in a messy fashion when dropped into the water. The secret is to use the freshest of eggs. A drop of vinegar in the water also helps, but do not add salt as this encourages the egg white to break up and defeats the purpose. (This is why you do add a pinch of salt when beating egg whites.)

450 g/ 1 lb MASHED POTATOES
   (MADE FROM ABOUT 675 g/ 1½ lb
   UNCOOKED POTATOES)
2 SPRING ONIONS, TRIMMED AND
   FINELY CHOPPED
7 VERY FRESH EGGS
½ tsp SALT
115 g/ 4 oz FLOUR
1 tsp BAKING POWDER
1 tsp VINEGAR
about 150 ml/ ¼ pt HOLLANDAISE SAUCE
   (SEE PAGE 20)
PEPPER
VEGETABLE OIL, FOR FRYING

In a large bowl, mix the mashed potatoes with the chopped spring onions, 1 of the eggs, lightly beaten, the salt and a good twist of black pepper.

Mix the flour and baking powder and add enough of this, holding a little back, to make a not-too-sticky dough with the consistency of a scone mixture. If too moist, add a little more of the flour mixture.

Roll the dough out to a thickness of about 1 cm/½ in and then use a 8.5 cm/3½ in diameter pastry cutter to cut out 6 cakes, re-rolling the trimmings if necessary.

Heat a little oil over a low heat and fry the cakes for about 5 minutes on each side, until golden brown and cooked through. The outsides should be crispy, but the insides will still be soft and a bit mushy. Keep them warm.

Meanwhile, three-quarters fill a frying pan with water and add the vinegar. Bring just to a simmer over a gentle heat. Working in batches of no more than 2, poach the remaining eggs by dropping them into the water in the frying pan.

As soon as they are cooked to taste, remove them from the pan with a fish slice. Drain them well and keep them warm in a covered dish while cooking the rest.

Place a hot potato cake on each plate. Top each with a poached egg, pour over some warm Hollandaise Sauce and serve immediately.

FROMAGE FRAIS WITH MELON PURÉE

Fromage frais is a delicious bland-tasting fresh cheese which has always been popular in France but has recently caught on in other countries and is becoming almost as popular as yogurt. Available in supermarkets, it comes with various different fat contents – even the 0% fat version tastes wonderfully creamy.

The mild flavour of fromage frais makes it incredibly versatile in the kitchen. As well as being used in cooking, it can be eaten just as it is as an alternative to cream cheese or double cream, used as a base for dips and sauces, or served with fresh fruit, fruit sauces and purées for breakfast or desserts.

675 g/ 1½ lb MELON FLESH
   (1 MEDIUM MELON SHOULD
   SUFFICE)
1 tsp GROUND GINGER
450 g/ 1 lb FROMAGE FRAIS
CHOPPED STEM GINGER, FRESH MINT,
   LEMON BALM LEAVES OR
   EDIBLE FLOWERS, TO GARNISH
   (OPTIONAL)

Purée the melon flesh with the ginger in a blender or food processor and chill for at least 2 hours, or preferably overnight.

Divide the fromage frais between 6 dishes or bowls (glass looks nice) and pour over the melon purée. Garnish with the chopped stem ginger, leaves or flowers, if using.

Al Fresco Fare

This menu is designed for outdoor entertaining, with all the dishes easily prepared in advance to be served cold. It is always fun to entertain 'al fresco', whether it be simply on a table in the back garden, the perfect picnic at Glyndebourne or even – as the saying goes – 'if wet, in the village hall'.

**GOLDEN MUSHROOM CREAM TART
CHEESE, ONION AND SWEETCORN
FLAN**

**SALADE RUSSE
BEETROOT WITH SOUR CREAM
AND HERBS
GREEK SALAD**

**CHOCOLATE BROWNIES WITH
HONEYED CRÈME FRAÎCHE AND
BERRIES**

GOLDEN MUSHROOM CREAM TART

This recipe was given to me by Ursula Ferrigno, a brilliant and innovative vegetarian cook who teaches at the excellent Vegetarian Society Cookery School in Altrincham, Cheshire.

Ursula is Italian by descent and specializes in teaching regional Italian vegetarian dishes, the list of which is endless. After all, Italians very often cook and enjoy vegetable-based dishes whether or not they are vegetarian.

I always imagined that I didn't like wholemeal pastry – as it is so often hard, heavy and tasteless – until I tried this recipe, which produces light crispy, crumbly and buttery results.

For the pastry
115 g/ 4 oz WHOLEMEAL FLOUR
1 tsp BAKING POWDER
GOOD PINCH OF SALT
1 tsp BROWN SUGAR
55 g/ 2 oz BUTTER
2 tsp OLIVE OIL
For the filling
4 tbsp OLIVE OIL
1 WHOLE HEAD OF GARLIC, CLOVES
    PEELED BUT LEFT WHOLE
2 ONIONS, CHOPPED
1 tbsp CHOPPED PARSLEY
¼ tsp PAPRIKA
30 g/ 1 oz BUTTER
225 g/ 8 oz MUSHROOMS, SLICED
4 tbsp GREEK-STYLE YOGURT OR
    FROMAGE FRAIS
1 EGG, BEATEN
SALT AND PEPPER

First make the pastry: put the dry ingredients in a bowl, then rub in the butter until the mixture resembles fine breadcrumbs. Mix in 3 tablespoons of cold water with the oil until a dough forms. (I make mine in a food processor.) Chill for at least 30 minutes.

Roll out the chilled pastry and use to line a 23 cm/9 in loose-bottomed flan tin. Chill until needed.

Now make the filling: heat half the oil in a small heavy-based saucepan over a moderate heat and sauté the garlic cloves for 3 minutes, stirring frequently.

Add 300 ml/½ pt water and season with salt and pepper. Cover and simmer for 45 minutes, then purée the contents of the saucepan in a blender or food processor.

Preheat the oven to 200C/400F/gas6.

Heat the remaining oil over a very low heat in a heavy-based pan which has a lid and sauté the onions and parsley, stirring frequently, for 10 minutes.

Cover with the lid and cook for 15 minutes more, stirring occasionally. Add the paprika, season with salt and pepper and stir in the garlic purée. Cook this over a high heat, stirring, for 2–3 minutes until reduced to a thick creamy sauce.

Melt the butter in a frying pan over a moderate heat and stir-fry the mushrooms for 5–10 minutes, or until completely soft. Season with salt and pepper and stir in 1 tablespoon of the yogurt or fromage frais.

Mix the remaining yogurt or fromage frais with the beaten egg and season with salt and pepper.

Bake the pastry case blind for 5 minutes. Then spread the mushroom mixture over the bottom of the case, cover this with the onion and garlic sauce and pour the egg mixture over this. Return to the oven and bake for 20 minutes.

Serve hot, warm or cold.

CHEESE, ONION AND SWEETCORN FLAN

The filling for this old-fashioned flan is less rich than a classic quiche filling, using fewer eggs and milk instead of cream. None the less, it is creamy in texture and savoury tasting – and costs considerably less to make!

This quantity will provide 6 slices as part of a buffet, but would provide 4 good main-course helpings.

225 g/ 8 oz SHORTCRUST PASTRY
    (SEE PAGE 18)
55 g/ 2 oz BUTTER
2 LARGE ONIONS, CHOPPED
1 tsp MUSTARD POWDER
1 rounded tbsp FLOUR
300 ml/ ½ pt MILK
55 g/ 2 oz FARMHOUSE CHEDDAR OR
    OTHER TASTY HARD
    CHEESE, GRATED
1 EGG, LIGHTLY BEATEN
115 g/ 4 oz SWEETCORN KERNELS,
    DRAINED IF CANNED OR DEFROSTED
    IF FROZEN
SALT AND PEPPER

Preheat the oven to 200C/400F/gas6.

Roll out the pastry and use it to line a 23 cm/9 in loose-bottomed flan tin. Chill while making the filling.

Melt the butter in a saucepan over a moderate heat and cook the onions for 5–10 minutes, stirring constantly, until soft and golden.

Add the mustard and flour, mix well then add the milk and bring to the boil, stirring constantly. Turn down the heat and simmer gently for 2–3 minutes.

Add the cheese, then remove the pan from the heat and allow it to cool for 2–3 minutes. Stir in the egg and sweetcorn and season with salt and pepper.

Pour into the pastry case and bake for 30–40 minutes, or until the filling is set and the top golden.

SALADE RUSSE

The mere thought of Russian salad used to conjure up childhood memories of something horrid out of a tin which appeared on 'plate salads', until I read four short lines while browsing through a Victorian cookbook I found in a junk shop in Australia. On reading the description of Russian salad to be found on page 87 of the 'Berrambool Cookbook' by a certain Mrs Alured Kelly, I realized that, home-made, it could be no less than delicious – and thoroughly deserves a revival. There follow Mrs Kelly's directions:

'Ingredients: peas, French beans, carrots, asparagus, small potatoes in equal quantities all nicely cooked. Mix well with mayonnaise sauce.'

BEETROOT WITH SOUR CREAM AND HERBS

This quick and easy salad with a difference is quite special enough to serve as a cold first course. It looks quite stunning, with the bright green of the fresh herbs against the pinks and purples of the beetroot. Use whatever herbs are available, such as parsley, dill, chives, tarragon, coriander, basil or marjoram.

250 g/ 8½ oz COOKED
   BEETROOT, DICED
3 heaped tbsp SOUR CREAM OR
   GREEK-STYLE YOGURT
2 tbsp CHOPPED FRESH HERBS
   (SEE ABOVE)
SALT AND PEPPER

Put the beetroot in a bowl and mix in the cream or yogurt. Season to taste with salt and pepper.

Transfer to a serving dish and sprinkle with herbs.

Serve at room temperature or chilled.

GREEK SALAD

Anyone who has been to Greece in the summer will be very familiar with this filling savoury salad. To me, it is one of the few foreign dishes which tastes better at home!

After being served it at almost every meal on a small Greek island one summer I began to hate it. Once back home, however, I soon started to prepare it myself to remind me of the brilliant blue sky and sea and the dazzling whitewashed houses of the Aegean.

This really is a summer salad, so it is simply not worth bothering to make it unless you can get really ripe tasty tomatoes.

If you make the salad in advance and keep it in the fridge, take it out at least 30 minutes before serving as it tastes much better served at room temperature. If you want to serve this as a substantial main course, simply double the quantities.

225 g/ 8 oz TOMATOES, SLICED,
   ROUGHLY CHOPPED OR CUT INTO
   SMALL WEDGES
225 g/ 8 oz FETA CHEESE, ROUGHLY
   CHOPPED OR CRUMBLED
½ CUCUMBER, SLICED OR CUT INTO
   BITE-SIZED CHUNKS
1 MILD ONION, SLICED
1 RED, GREEN OR YELLOW SWEET
   PEPPER, DESEEDED AND
   CHOPPED (OPTIONAL)
85 g/ 3 oz BLACK OLIVES
3 tbsp FRUITY EXTRA VIRGIN
   OLIVE OIL
SALT AND PEPPER
6 LEMON WEDGES, TO SERVE

Place the the tomatoes, cheese, cucumber, onion, pepper if using, and the olives in a bowl. Season with salt and pepper and pour over the oil. Toss well.

Arrange the lemon slices on top of the salad. Each person squeezes her or his own lemon juice over the salad according to taste.

CHOCOLATE BROWNIES WITH HONEYED CRÈME FRAÎCHE AND BERRIES

There are endless variations on recipes for chocolate brownies: some sticky and fudgy, some more spongy; some have nuts, some have fruit; some are iced and some are not. This version is light and spongy, with a few walnut pieces for crunch. It makes a good plain cake for tea, or may be served as it is here, as a luxurious dessert to round off a special menu.

Crème fraîche is available in most delicatessens and large supermarkets. If you can't find any, substitute sour cream or double cream.

115 g/ 4 oz UNSALTED BUTTER,
   PLUS MORE FOR GREASING
115 g/ 4 oz FLOUR, PLUS
   MORE FOR COATING
100 g/ 3½ oz PLAIN
   CHOCOLATE, MELTED
¼ tsp BICARBONATE OF SODA
¼ tsp SALT
115 g/ 4 oz SUGAR
2 LARGE (SIZE 1) EGGS
½ tsp VANILLA ESSENCE
3 tbsp MILK
55 g/ 2 oz CHOPPED WALNUTS
To serve
150 ml/ ¼ pt CRÈME FRAÎCHE
   (SEE ABOVE)
1 tbsp RUNNY HONEY
350 g/ 12 oz BERRIES OR OTHER
   FRESH FRUIT IN SEASON

Preheat the oven to 180C/350F/gas4. Grease a 20 cm/8 in square cake tin or other suitably sized cake tin with butter and coat it with flour.

Melt the chocolate in a bowl set over a pan of hot water (or in a microwave) and then allow it to cool.

Sift the flour, bicarbonate of soda and the salt together on to a sheet of grease-proof paper.

In a bowl, cream the butter and sugar until light and fluffy. (I use a hand-held electric whisk.) Beat in the eggs, one at a time, followed by the vanilla. Beat well and then beat in the cooled melted chocolate.

Beat in alternating thirds of the sifted flour mixture and the milk until they are all mixed in. Then mix in the chopped nuts.

Pour the batter into the prepared tin and bake for 30–35 minutes, or until a skewer inserted into the centre of the cake comes out clean.

Run a knife around the edge of the tin and turn the cake out on a wire rack to cool. When cool, cut it into 6 equal portions.

To serve: place a piece of brownie on each plate. Whip the cream with the honey and then spoon this over or along-side the brownie and add some fruit.

An International Affair

This eclectic dinner-party menu brings together inspiration from France, Italy, the USA and Australia to produce a memorable meal which will impress any guest – however sophisticated and well-travelled – without you having to spend hours in the kitchen.

FRENCH ONION SOUP

CABBAGE GÂTEAU
SWEET POTATO HASH
CARROTS BRAISED IN OLIVE OIL
WITH ROSEMARY AND GARLIC

FRESH PEACH PAVLOVA

FRENCH ONION SOUP

This well-loved classic is perhaps most famous for having been enjoyed in the small hours by night revellers and market porters alike in the Paris cafés which surrounded the vegetable market of Les Halles.

The authentic way to serve this homely comforting soup is to place the bread and cheese in the bottom of each bowl before pouring in the hot soup. I prefer my bread less soggy and like to float it on top. I also prefer the taste of the cheese when grilled.

55 g/ 2 oz BUTTER

1 tbsp VEGETABLE OIL

675 g/ 1½ lb ONIONS,
   THINLY SLICED

1 heaped tbsp FLOUR

1.5 litres/ 2½ pt VEGETABLE
   STOCK

6 SLICES OF FRENCH BREAD

55 g/ 2 oz EMMENTAL OR GRUYÈRE
   CHEESE, GRATED

SALT AND PEPPER

In a large saucepan, melt the butter with the oil over a very low heat and cook the onions, stirring occasionally, for 20–30 minutes, or until soft and brown but not burned.

Add the flour, stir well and cook for 1 minute more.

Stir the stock in thoroughly, cover and simmer for 20 minutes. Season to taste.

While the soup is simmering, preheat a hot grill.

Just before serving, toast the French bread slices lightly on both sides. Top one side of each with grated cheese, return them to the grill and cook until the cheese bubbles.

Pour the soup into warm bowls, float one of the cheese toasts on top of each bowl and serve immediately.

CABBAGE GÂTEAU

Though quick and easy to make, the spectacular appearance of this savoury 'cake' makes it perfect for a special dinner party.

If you can't find fresh dill, substitute the same quantity of tarragon, parsley, chervil or chives. If you don't have any pine kernels, substitute chopped walnuts, peanuts or cashews.

3 tbsp OLIVE OIL, PLUS MORE
   FOR GREASING

225 g/ 8 oz CABBAGE (ANY KIND),
   FINELY CHOPPED, PLUS 6 LARGE
   CABBAGE LEAVES

2 ONIONS, CHOPPED

3 GARLIC CLOVES, CRUSHED

225 g/ 8 oz MUSHROOMS, CHOPPED

225 g/ 8 oz AUBERGINE, COARSELY
   DICED INTO PIECES ABOUT
   6 mm/ ¼ in

55 g/ 2 oz PINE KERNELS
   (SEE ABOVE)

115 g/ 4 oz FRESH BREADCRUMBS
   (BROWN OR WHITE)

SALT AND PEPPER

3 EGGS

225 g/ 8 oz RICOTTA CHEESE

1 tbsp FINELY CHOPPED FRESH DILL
   (SEE ABOVE)

Preheat the oven to 200C/400F/gas 6 and grease a 20 cm/8 in cake tin with a little oil.

Blanch the large whole cabbage leaves in a large pan of boiling salted water for 5 minutes. Drain, then plunge them into a bowl of very cold water to refresh them. Drain and pat dry on tea towels or paper towels.

Using a sharp knife, cut away the thick central stem level with the leaf. Line the bottom and sides of the prepared cake tin with the cabbage leaves, leaving enough of each sticking above the rim of the tin to fold over and cover the filling.

LEFT TO RIGHT: *French Onion Soup, Cabbage Gâteau and Carrots Braised in Olive Oil with Rosemary and Garlic*

Heat the oil in a heavy-based saucepan over a moderate heat and cook the onion, garlic and mushrooms, stirring frequently, for 10–15 minutes or until soft. Tip the contents of the pan into a bowl and mix in the chopped cabbage, aubergine, pine kernels and breadcrumbs and season well with salt and pepper.

Allow this to cool for a minute or two, then beat 2 of the eggs and blend them thoroughly into the mixture.

In another bowl, thoroughly beat the cheese with the remaining egg and the herbs and season with salt and pepper. (I do this in a food processor.)

Pack half the cabbage mixture into the lined cake tin. Smooth the Ricotta mixture over this to make a central layer, then cover with the remaining cabbage mixture. Fold over the overhanging cabbage leaves to enclose the 'gâteau' completely.

Cover the tin with foil and bake for 1 hour.

Turn out and serve hot, cut in wedges.

SWEET POTATO HASH

This simple recipe is a classic American favourite. Orange-fleshed sweet potatoes are distinguished by their russet-brown skin, while that of the less flavourful white-fleshed variety is beetrooty-purple.

1.35 k/ 3 lb ORANGE-FLESHED
  SWEET POTATOES IN THEIR SKINS
170 g/ 6 oz UNSALTED BUTTER
SALT AND PEPPER

Preheat the oven to 180C/350F/gas4 and bake the sweet potatoes in their skins for 45 minutes.

Meanwhile clarify the butter by melting it in a small saucepan over a low heat. Allow it to cool and settle for about 1 minute. Then carefully pour it off into a bowl, leaving the unwanted solids in the pan.

When the sweet potatoes are cool enough to handle, peel off their skins and discard them. Cut the flesh into 2.5 cm/1 in cubes.

Heat the butter in a large frying pan or wok over a moderate heat and stir-fry the sweet potato cubes for 5–10 minutes, until crispy and golden.

Season with salt and pepper, transfer to a warmed serving dish and serve immediately.

CARROTS BRAISED IN OLIVE OIL WITH ROSEMARY AND GARLIC

The long slow cooking of this easy recipe transforms a simple root vegetable into a very tasty dish, which may also be served hot or cold as a first course.

3 tbsp EXTRA VIRGIN OLIVE OIL
675 g/ 1½ lb CARROTS, CUT INTO
  SMALL STICKS
2 GARLIC CLOVES, CRUSHED
JUICE AND THIN STRIP OF FINELY
  PARED ZEST FROM AN UNWAXED
  LEMON, ABOUT 7.5 cm/ 3 in LONG
1 tbsp FINELY CHOPPED FRESH
  ROSEMARY OR 1½ tsp DRIED
SALT AND PEPPER
SPRIG OF ROSEMARY, TO GARNISH
  (OPTIONAL)

Put all the ingredients in a heavy-based saucepan covered with a tight-fitting lid, but reserving half the lemon juice.

Cook over the lowest possible heat for 1 hour, stirring occasionally.

Just before serving remove the strip of lemon zest and stir in the remaining lemon juice. Garnish with a rosemary sprig, if using.

FRESH PEACH PAVLOVA

This gorgeous gooey confection of meringue and cream, named after the famous ballerina while she was on a trip 'down under', is always a sure-fire success as a spectacular party pudding. Made with fresh peaches it comes near to perfection.

Use the leftover egg yolks to make the Cappuccino Ice-cream on page 115.

Serves 6–10

6 EGG WHITES
300 g/ 10½ oz CASTER SUGAR
PINCH OF SALT
1½ tbsp VINEGAR
300 ml/ ½ pt DOUBLE
  CREAM, WHIPPED
6 SMALL OR 4 LARGE PEACHES,
  PEELED, STONED AND
  THINLY SLICED

Preheat the oven to 150C/300F/gas2.

Cut 4 circles with a diameter of 23 cm/9 in from greaseproof paper. Place a circle in each of two loose-bottomed sandwich cake tins of the same size. Wet one side of each of the remaining circles and place them, wet side down, on the first circles. (The water sandwiched between the papers makes it easier to remove the paper when the meringues are cooked.)

Beat the egg whites with half the sugar, the salt and the vinegar until very stiff. Add the rest of the sugar and beat again until stiff and glossy.

Spread the meringue on the paper circles, leaving a border about 2.5 cm/1 in clear of the edge. Bake for 30 minutes, then lower the heat to 130C/275F/gas1 and bake for 30 minutes more.

Remove the meringues from the tins and allow them to cool. Invert and carefully peel off the paper.

Place one meringue circle on a serving plate and spread with half the cream. Arrange half the peach slices on this. Place the remaining meringue circle on top and then spread it with the remaining cream and arrange the rest of the peach slices in concentric circles over it (like a French apple tart).

Cook-ahead Cuisine

For mid-week entertaining, or other occasions when the busy cook has little time before the guests arrive for a meal, here is a menu in which most of the recipes can be prepared the day before and involve the minimum of last-minute cooking.

VERY GARLICKY VEGETABLE SOUP

PASTA-STUFFED PEPPERS
LEAF SALAD

JOAN'S SPICE CAKE WITH SEVEN-MINUTE BROWN SUGAR FROSTING

VERY GARLICKY VEGETABLE SOUP

This chunky rustic vegetable soup is so tasty it will vanish in no time, yet it is simplicity itself to make. Don't chicken out (if you will excuse the meatist expression) and use less garlic – the initial blanching removes any harshness and, thus treated, the garlic gives the most wonderful rich flavour to the finished soup.

16 GARLIC CLOVES

3 tbsp OLIVE OIL

1 LARGE ONION, CHOPPED,

2 LARGE LEEKS, COARSELY
   CHOPPED (INCLUDING GOOD BITS
   OF GREEN)

2 LARGE CARROTS,
   COARSELY CHOPPED

2 LARGE CELERY STICKS,
   COARSELY CHOPPED

225 g/ 8 oz SWEDE, CUT INTO BITE-
   SIZED CHUNKS

450 g/ 1 lb POTATOES, CUT INTO
   BITE-SIZED CHUNKS

1.75 litres/ 3 pt VEGETABLE
   STOCK

225 g/ 8 oz GREEN CABBAGE (ANY
   KIND), SHREDDED

225 g/ 8 oz TOMATOES,
   COARSELY CHOPPED

SALT AND PEPPER

FRUITY EXTRA VIRGIN OLIVE OIL,
   TO SERVE (OPTIONAL)

Put the garlic cloves in a small saucepan and cover them with cold water. Bring to the boil, drain and discard the water. Cover again with cold water, bring to the boil again and then drain and discard water. Repeat the process for a third time and then set the blanched garlic aside.

Heat the oil in a very large saucepan over a moderate heat and cook the onion for 5–10 minutes, stirring occasionally, until softened and just beginning to turn golden. Add the leeks, carrots, celery, swede, potatoes and blanched garlic and continue to cook for 5 minutes, stirring constantly.

Add the stock and bring to the boil. Cover the pan and simmer over a very low heat for 15 minutes.

Add the cabbage and tomatoes, cover once more and continue to simmer for 15 more minutes. Check that all the vegetables are quite tender. Adjust the seasoning if necessary (don't forget the stock will already be quite strongly seasoned).

Serve in warmed bowls or dishes, accompanied by crusty bread. Don't feel you need to add chopped herbs or swirls of cream as this soup simply doesn't need it – its beauty lies in its fresh simplicity. A drizzle of olive oil, however, would not be gilding the lily.

Very Garlicky Vegetable Soup

PASTA-STUFFED PEPPERS

This is a lovely variation on the classic stuffed-vegetable theme, and proves a more substantial main dish than those with the more usual rice-based stuffings. Any type of pasta will do: shells, twizzles, macaroni etc.

Sun-dried tomatoes preserved in oil are available in small jars from delicatessens.

6 LARGE RED OR YELLOW SWEET PEPPERS, HALVED LENGTHWISE AND DESEEDED

4 tbsp DRAINED AND CHOPPED SUN-DRIED TOMATOES IN OIL (SEE ABOVE), OIL RESERVED FOR GREASING

55 g/ 2 oz BUTTER

3 ONIONS, CHOPPED

2 tbsp FLOUR

450 ml/ ¾ pt MILK

115 g/ 4 oz GRATED EMMENTAL OR GRUYÈRE CHEESE

1 heaped tsp DRIED HERBES DE PROVENCE

170 g/ 6 oz COOKED PASTA SHAPES (SEE ABOVE)

SALT AND PEPPER

85 g/ 3 oz GRATED FRESH PARMESAN CHEESE

Preheat the oven to 180C/350F/gas4 and with a little of the oil from the sun-dried tomatoes lightly grease a shallow ovenproof dish or baking tin big enough to take the 12 pepper halves in one layer.

Bring a large pan of salted water to the boil and blanch the pepper halves in it for 3 minutes. Drain them, refresh in cold water and drain again. Leave them, cut side down, on paper towels to drain thoroughly until needed.

Meanwhile, melt the butter in a sauce-pan and cook the onions over the lowest possible heat for about 20 minutes, stirring occasionally, until they are very soft and pale golden.

Stir in the flour, turn up the heat to moderate and cook for 1–2 minutes, stirring constantly. Add the milk and bring to the boil. Turn down the heat and simmer, stirring constantly, for 2–3 minutes or until thick and creamy.

Add the grated Emmental or Gruyère, the dried herbs and the sun-dried tomatoes. Season to taste and continue to cook, stirring, for 2–3 minutes, until the cheese is melted. Stir the cooked pasta into the sauce and pile this mixture into the drained pepper halves.

Arrange the stuffed pepper halves in the prepared dish or tin. Sprinkle over the Parmesan and bake for 40–45 minutes, or until the stuffing is bubbling and golden.

Serve 2 pepper halves per person.

LEAF SALAD

With the vogue for exotic mixtures of ingredients in salad first courses, plain salads seem to have gone rather out of fashion. Yet nothing could be nicer to serve on its own after a main course than a simple salad of fresh tender leaves dressed with a classic vinaigrette.

Now that most supermarkets sell a wonderful selection of ready-trimmed and washed mixed salad leaves in various varieties, this could not be simpler to prepare. A few fresh herbs snipped over the leaves just before dressing makes a nice change, or you might like to add a small crushed clove of garlic to the dressing.

4 tbsp VINAIGRETTE (SEE PAGE 18)
**115 g/ 4 oz PREPARED SALAD
    LEAVES OF CHOICE**

Just before sitting down to the meal, pour the dressing into the bottom of a roomy bowl. Place the salad servers (or whatever is to be used to serve the salad) in the bowl over the dressing and then tip in the leaves. The salad servers will keep the dressing away from the leaves (as it might otherwise make them go limp if the salad sits too long) until it is time to eat the salad.

At the last moment, toss the salad well before serving.

JOAN'S SPICE CAKE WITH SEVEN-MINUTE BROWN SUGAR FROSTING

Joan Campbell is the Food Editor of Vogue Australia *magazine and is one of the best and most innovative cooks in the world. Luckily she is a good friend and occasionally gives me recipes like this delicious easy and foolproof cake, which – amazingly – contains no eggs at all.*

If served on the day it is made, it has a light, fluffy and crumbly texture; if left for a day or two, it changes completely and becomes moist and fudgy. I like it both ways.

The frosting is based on an old-fashioned American recipe and has an intriguing soft, marshmallow-like texture.

170 g/ 6 oz RAISINS
**170 g/ 6 oz SOFT BROWN SUGAR
    (LIGHT OR DARK)**
250 g/ 8½ oz UNSALTED BUTTER
1 tsp VANILLA ESSENCE
**325 g/ 11 oz FLOUR, PLUS MORE
    FOR DUSTING**
1 tsp GROUND GINGER
½ tsp GROUND CINNAMON
½ tsp GROUND CLOVES
½ tsp GROUND MIXED SPICE
¼ tsp SALT
1 tsp BICARBONATE OF SODA
OIL, FOR GREASING
For the frosting
**140 g/ 5 oz SOFT BROWN SUGAR (LIGHT
    OR DARK)**
⅛ tsp GROUND MACE
PINCH OF SALT
⅛ tsp CREAM OF TARTAR
1 tsp VANILLA ESSENCE
WHITE OF 1 LARGE (SIZE 1) EGG

Preheat the oven to 190C/375F/gas5. Oil and flour a 2.25 litre/4 pt ring-shaped cake tin.

Place the raisins, sugar and butter in a saucepan with 350 ml/12 fl oz water. Bring to the boil, turn down the heat and simmer for 5 minutes. Allow to cool completely, then stir in the vanilla essence.

Sieve the flour into a large bowl and add the spices, salt and bicarbonate of soda. Mix well, pour in the liquid ingredients and beat quickly but thoroughly until well amalgamated.

Pour the mixture into the prepared tin and bake for 45 minutes, or until a skewer inserted into the cake comes out dry. Turn out on a wire rack and allow to cool.

Meanwhile, make the frosting: place all the ingredients in a bowl together with 2 tablespoons of water and set over a pan of boiling water. Whisk the contents of the bowl with an electric whisk for 3 minutes, then remove the bowl from the pan and whisk for 4 more minutes as the frosting cools.

Cover the cooled cake roughly with the frosting.

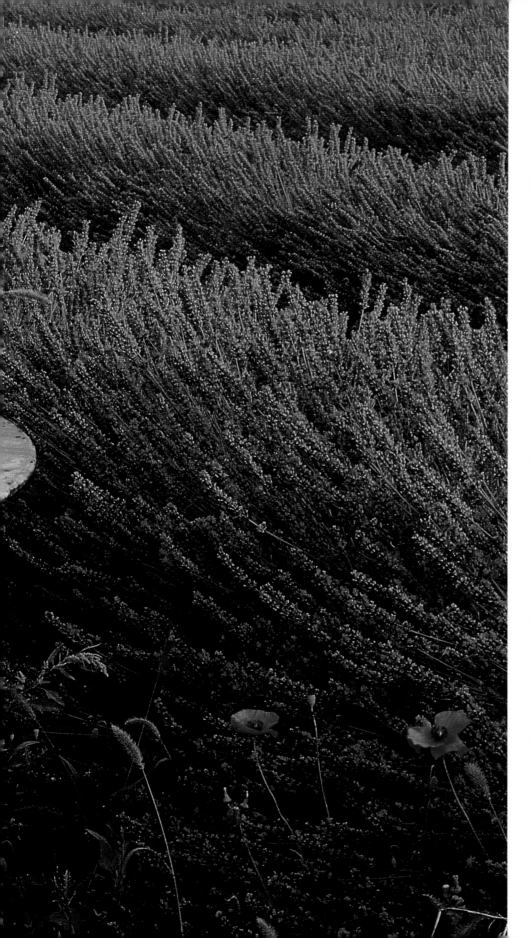

The Fruits of the Fields

This fresh and summery menu celebrates the skills of the market gardener and is a veritable cornucopia of vegetables, herbs and flowers. Enjoy this meal indoors or out, in winter or summer; whenever or wherever, it will conjure up an atmosphere of open fields and countryside, fresh air and sunshine.

FRESH TOMATO SOUP

ARTICHOKES WITH HOLLANDAISE SAUCE

GARDENER'S LASAGNE

LAVENDER, HONEY AND GIN ICE-CREAM
YUULONG LAVENDER BISCUITS

FRESH TOMATO SOUP

One of the nicest and easiest of all soups, I make this only when really good ripe tasty tomatoes are available. Don't fall into the trap of thinking that if it's 'only soup' you are making, second-grade vegetables will do. Certainly it doesn't matter if the tomatoes are a little over-ripe and squashy, but Dutch hothouse tomatoes with no flavour will only produce a boring tasteless soup.

If you want to serve this soup for a posh occasion, you could remove the skins from the tomatoes, but I never do. If you have no basil, use tarragon or parsley.

2 tbsp OLIVE OIL
2 ONIONS, THINLY SLICED
675 g/ 1½ lb REALLY RIPE
   TOMATOES, CHOPPED
1.75 litres/ 3¾ pt VEGETABLE
   STOCK
SALT AND PEPPER
FRESH BASIL LEAVES, TO GARNISH
   (SEE ABOVE)

Heat the oil in a medium-sized pan which has a lid. Add the onion, cover the pan and cook over the lowest possible heat for about 20 minutes, shaking the pan occasionally. The onions must be completely soft, sweet and dark golden brown.

Add the chopped tomatoes and the stock. Bring to the boil, reduce the heat and simmer for 3–4 minutes. (The tomatoes should not be cooked for too long to ensure they retain a nice fresh taste.) Adjust the seasoning, if necessary.

Serve in warmed bowls, sprinkled with herbs.

ARTICHOKES WITH HOLLANDAISE SAUCE

Artichokes are traditionally served either hot or cold. If served cold, they should not be chilled but at room temperature, and are best accompanied by either a vinaigrette dressing or mayonnaise (with garlic if you like). Hot they may be served simply with melted butter, with Hollandaise Sauce or a Beurre Blanc (see pages 20–21).

Cooking artichokes could not be simpler, but eating them is a little more complicated if you have never tried one before and no one has ever explained the pleasant ritual. This is what you do:

Starting with the outside leaves, pull them off one by one. There is a little bit of soft edible 'flesh' at the bottom of each one. Dip this in your chosen sauce, then scrape it off into your mouth with the front teeth. Discard the leaf. (Don't forget to place a large receptacle in the middle of the table for the debris.) Continue until all the leaves have been dealt with. You will now be left with the artichoke bottom, which is the best part. To get at this, however, you must first remove the little brush of chokes which grow from its top. Fingers and a knife are needed here. Discard the choke hairs and then enjoy the wonderful meaty base using a knife and fork, finishing up the remains of the sauce.

6 ARTICHOKES (THE ONES FROM
   BRITTANY ARE BY FAR THE BEST
   IF YOU CAN GET THEM)
ABOUT 300 ml/ ½ pt WARM HOLLANDAISE
   SAUCE (SEE PAGE 20)

Unless you have an enormous pan you will need to fill two of your biggest pans with salted water. (The water will need to come halfway up the artichokes.) Bring to the boil.

Cut away the stem of each vegetable as close to the bottom as possible. Then arrange the artichokes, bottoms down, in the boiling water. Cover with a lid and simmer for 45 minutes.

Remove the cooked artichokes from the pan and drain them upside down for a few minutes. (I stack them in a row on the plate rack over my draining board.)

Serve immediately with the warm Hollandaise Sauce, or leave to cool.

GARDENER'S LASAGNE

This baked pasta dish, with its three layers of different vegetables and rich cheese sauce, is easily as good as the traditional meat-based version – even the most hardened carnivore will be asking for more.

Many people swear by the kind of dried lasagne which needs no pre-cooking. I find it most unsatisfactory and a very poor substitute for the traditional kind, which after all only takes 8–9 minutes to cook, while you are preparing the rest of the dish.

If you want this recipe to be more substantial, cook 3 more sheets of lasagne and put them in the bottom of the dish.

9 SHEETS OF TRADITIONAL DRIED
   LASAGNE (SEE ABOVE), WEIGHING
   ABOUT 170 g/ 6 oz IN TOTAL
SALT AND PEPPER
OLIVE OIL, FOR GREASING
For the sauce
55 g/ 2 oz BUTTER
55 g/ 2 oz FLOUR
700 ml/ 1¼ pt MILK
140 g/ 5 oz GRATED EMMENTAL
   CHEESE
SCRAPE OF NUTMEG
For filling 1
1 tbsp OLIVE OIL
225 g/ 8 oz MUSHROOMS, SLICED
1 tsp CHOPPED THYME OR
   ½ tsp DRIED
For filling 2
3 tbsp OLIVE OIL
1 LARGE AUBERGINE, WEIGHING
   ABOUT 285 g/ 10 oz, CUT ACROSS
   INTO 1 cm/ ½ in SLICES
For filling 3
1 tbsp OLIVE OIL
1 ONION, CHOPPED
2 GARLIC CLOVES, FINELY CHOPPED
225 g/ 8 oz FRESH SPINACH

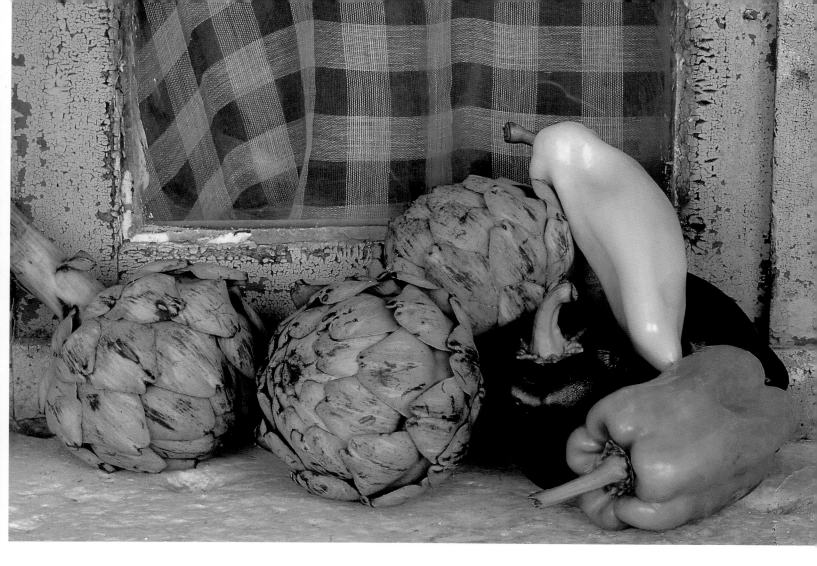

Preheat the oven to 200C/400F/gas6. Oil a baking sheet and a shallow oven-proof dish about 30 × 20 cm/12 × 8 in.

Cook the lasagne in a large pan of boiling salted water, according to the instructions on the packet, until tender but still very firm. Drain well.

Meanwhile, make the sauce: melt the butter in a saucepan over a moderate heat and add the flour. Cook this roux, stirring, for 2–3 minutes. Add 575 ml/ 1 pt of the milk and bring to the boil, stirring constantly (I use a balloon whisk). When the sauce has thickened, turn down the heat to low and simmer, stirring constantly, for 3–4 minutes.

Add 115 g/4 oz of the cheese, season with salt and pepper and nutmeg. Cook for 2–3 minutes more, stirring, or until

the cheese has melted and the sauce is smooth. Remove from the heat and stir in the remaining milk.

Make filling 1: heat the oil in a frying pan over a moderate heat and stir-fry the mushrooms with the thyme for about 5 minutes, or until softened. Season with salt and pepper.

Make filling 2: arrange the aubergine slices in one layer on the prepared baking sheet and brush them with the oil. Season with salt and pepper and bake for about 15–20 minutes, or until softened and lightly browned.

Make filling 3: heat the oil in a wok or large frying pan over a moderate heat and stir-fry the onion for about 5 minutes or until soft and translucent, adding the garlic halfway through.

Add the spinach and season with salt and pepper. Turn up the heat and stir-fry for 1–2 minutes, or just until the leaves begin to wilt. Do not over-cook or the spinach will turn to a mush.

Assemble the lasagne: spread filling 1 over the bottom of the prepared dish, then pour over one-quarter of the sauce. Cover this with 3 sheets of lasagne. Spread these with filling 2, followed by another quarter of the sauce. Arrange 3 more sheets of lasagne over this, then cover with filling 3, followed by one-quarter of the sauce. Top with the remaining 3 sheets of lasagne and the remaining sauce.

Sprinkle with the remaining cheese and bake for about 30–40 minutes, or until bubbling and the top is golden.

YUULONG LAVENDER BISCUITS

Although I knew that lavender was often included in the popular herbes de Provence combination, I first became properly acquainted with the idea of flavouring food with lavender on a trip to Australia.

There I read an article about a lavender farm in Yuulong, near Melbourne, where they make lavender biscuits, Fascinated, I wrote to them for more details. It turns out that they make between thirteen and fourteen thousand of these biscuits each season, and they kindly sent me the recipe.

Makes 30
225 g/ 8 oz BUTTER (WELL WORTH USING BEST-QUALITY UNSALTED)
115 g/ 4 oz CASTER SUGAR
1 EGG, LIGHTLY BEATEN
170 g/ 6 oz SELF-RAISING FLOUR
1 tbsp DRIED LAVENDER FLOWERS

Preheat the oven to 180C/350F/gas4 and line a baking tray with non-stick baking paper.

Cream the butter with the sugar (I do this in my food processor). Add the egg and beat well. Add the flour and mix well, then finally mix in the flowers.

Place small teaspoonfuls of the mixture on the prepared baking tray, allowing space for them to spread. Bake for 15–20 minutes, or until the biscuits are pale golden in colour (be careful not to let them get too brown). They will not feel crisp to the touch until they have cooled.

Allow the biscuits to cool on a wire rack and store in an airtight container (if they ever last that long!).

LAVENDER, HONEY AND GIN ICE-CREAM

This type of ice-cream is particularly easy to make, as it doesn't need beating once you put it in the freezer.

Soft enough to serve straight from the freezer, it is delicious on its own but spectacular if served with lavender biscuits.

Makes 1.1 litres/ 2 pt
5 tbsp GIN
1 tbsp DRIED LAVENDER
6 EGG YOLKS
150 ml/ ¼ pt CLEAR HONEY (LAVENDER IF YOU CAN GET IT, OTHERWISE ANY GOOD-QUALITY FLOWER HONEY WILL DO)
300 ml/ ½ pt DOUBLE CREAM
ANY EDIBLE FLOWERS, TO GARNISH (OPTIONAL)

Warm the gin slightly in a small saucepan and then pour it over the lavender in a small bowl. Cover tightly with film and leave to infuse for 1 hour.

Strain the flavoured gin off through a fine sieve, pressing the lavender flowers against the sieve with the back of a spoon to extract all the flavour. Discard the flowers. You should end up with about 3 tablespoons of strongly flavoured gin. If it is a little under, top it up with a drop of plain gin.

In a large bowl, beat the egg yolks with a whisk (an electric whisk makes it much easier, otherwise use a wire balloon type), until very light and fluffy. In a small saucepan, heat the honey until just boiling.

Pour the hot honey in a thin steady stream over the egg yolks, whisking constantly. Keep whisking vigorously until the mixture has cooled and the yolks have increased in volume (this should take about 2–3 minutes using an electric whisk, but unfortunately at least 5–10 minutes by hand). Add the flavoured gin and stir to combine.

Whip the cream to soft peaks. Carefully fold it into the egg yolk mixture, blending well. Pour the mixture into a bowl or other suitable container and freeze for at least 8 hours.

Garnish with fresh flowers, if using, to serve.

Lavender, Honey and Gin Ice-cream with Yuulong Lavender Biscuits

Harvest Home

This menu has more than a hint of autumn, of mists and mellow fruitfulness. Containing a collection of full-blown flavours to satisfy the heartiest of appetites, it is a meal to celebrate a season of harvests safely gathered in — when the evenings are drawing in, sitting in the soft glow of candlelight, perhaps with a log crackling on the fire.

CREAM OF SCORCHED PEPPER SOUP

CHEESE AND ONION 'SAUSAGES'
YORKSHIRE PUDDINGS
MASHED POTATOES WITH OLIVES, OLIVE OIL AND PARMESAN
ONION AND SUN-DRIED TOMATO GRAVY
SEASONAL VEGETABLES

CODDLED PEARS IN SPICED RUM SAUCE

CREAM OF SCORCHED PEPPER SOUP

4 LARGE RIPE RED OR YELLOW
   SWEET PEPPERS
2 tbsp EXTRA VIRGIN OLIVE OIL
4 SHALLOTS OR 1 MEDIUM
   ONION, CHOPPED
1 tsp FRESH THYME LEAVES
   OR ½ tsp DRIED
2 GARLIC CLOVES, CRUSHED
1.1 litres/ 2 pt VEGETABLE
   STOCK
575 ml/ 1 pt MILK
SALT AND PEPPER
FRESH BASIL LEAVES OR OTHER
   HERBS, TO GARNISH

Preheat a hot grill.

Cut the peppers in quarters lengthwise and discard the seeds and any white membrane. Arrange the quarters, skin-side up, on the grill rack and grill until all the skin is blackened and blistered. Transfer to a plastic bag, close and leave for 5 minutes.

The blackened skins will now come away easily and can be discarded. Do not rinse the peppers or you will wash away the precious juices.

Meanwhile, heat the oil in a large heavy-based saucepan over a low heat and cook the shallots or onion, stirring occasionally, for 5–10 minutes, until soft and translucent.

Add the thyme, garlic, stock and all but one piece of the skinned peppers. Bring to the boil and simmer for 20 minutes.

Liquidize the mixture in a blender or food processor in batches and return to a clean pan. Add the milk, reheat and season to taste.

Cut the reserved piece of pepper into thin strips.

Pour the soup into 6 warmed bowls and garnish with the pepper strips and the fresh herbs.

CHEESE AND ONION 'SAUSAGES'

These incredibly tasty 'sausages' need not apologize for being a meat substitute, for they are quite good enough to stand up in their own right. Quick, easy and cheap to make, you can serve them as a main course with potatoes and vegetables. Set on a bed of chopped fresh tomatoes, dressed with a garlicky vinaigrette, they also make a good first course, lunch or supper dish.

Makes 6–8 sausages
115 g/ 4 oz STRONG CHEDDAR
   CHEESE, OR ANY OTHER TASTY
   HARD CHEESE, GRATED
170 g/ 6 oz FRESH WHITE
   BREADCRUMBS
1 SMALL MILD ONION, VERY
   FINELY CHOPPED
¼ tsp ENGLISH MUSTARD POWDER
1 tbsp CHOPPED PARSLEY
2 EGGS
4 tbsp MILK

SALT AND PEPPER
FLOUR, FOR COATING
OIL, FOR FRYING

In a bowl, mix the cheese, breadcrumbs, onion, mustard and parsley. Season well with salt and pepper.

Mix one whole egg and the yolk of the other (reserving the white) with the milk. Add this to the cheese mixture and mix well.

Form the mixture into 6 or 8 sausage shapes. Whisk the egg white lightly and dip the 'sausages' into it. Then roll them in flour, shaking off any excess.

Fry them in hot oil for about 10 minutes, turning occasionally so that they brown on all sides.

Cheese and Onion 'Sausages' with Yorkshire Puddings (page 70) and Onion and Sun-dried Tomato Gravy (page 70) served with seasonal vegetables

YORKSHIRE PUDDINGS

Why should something so totally delicious be reserved for meat eaters? Yorkshire puddings taste just as good without the roast beef. In fact, they were traditionally served on their own as a first course, to take the edge off appetites before the expensive meat course was brought to the table.

Probably the most traditional way of cooking Yorkshire pudding is in one big rectangular baking tray, cutting it into squares to serve it, but I prefer to cook mine in individual bun tins as this provides more crispy outside and less puddingy middle.

Makes 18–20 small puddings
115 g/ 4 oz PLAIN FLOUR
PINCH OF SALT
2 EGGS
300 ml/ ½ pt MILK (OR ROUGHLY
    EQUAL QUANTITIES MILK
    AND WATER)
2 tbsp VEGETABLE OIL

Sieve the flour with the salt into a bowl. Add the eggs and half the liquid. Beat well for 2–3 minutes.

Gradually add the remaining liquid and beat to incorporate. (All this can be done in seconds in a food processor.) Leave the batter to rest for about 1 hour.

Preheat the oven to 220C/425F/gas7.

Pour a few drops of oil into each section of 1 or 2 bun sheets. (If making one big pudding, use all the oil in a roasting tin measuring about 28 × 18 cm/ 11 × 7 in.) Place them in the preheated oven and leave until very hot (at least 5 minutes).

Beat the batter again briefly. Remove the sheet from the oven and, working as quickly as possible, put about 1 tablespoon of batter into as many sections as possible. Return to the oven for 15–20 minutes (30–40 minutes for a big one), until well risen and nice and brown.

Serve immediately.

MASHED POTATOES WITH OLIVES, OLIVE OIL AND PARMESAN

It isn't necessary to go all the way to Italy to eat good Italian food. Stephano Cavallini is the talented chef at the new, modern and very chic Halkin Hotel in London's Belgravia. He kindly gave me this recipe, which transforms a very English dish like mashed potatoes into a totally Mediterranean treat.

Signor Cavallini specifies the superb Raneira olive oil from just north of Imperia in Liguria. My own favourite 'luxury' oil, however, is Colonna, which is made in olive groves on the Adriatic coast opposite Rome. Both oils are available from good delicatessens.

These mashed potatoes are very rich and this recipe produces quite small helpings – double the quantities for hearty eaters!

675 g/ 1½ lb OLD POTATOES
2 tbsp EXTRA VIRGIN OLIVE OIL
    (SEE ABOVE)
1 tbsp SINGLE OR WHIPPING CREAM
30 g/ 1 oz STONED GREEN OLIVES,
    CUT INTO TINY STRIPS
30 g/ 1 oz STONED BLACK OLIVES,
    CUT INTO TINY STRIPS
30 g/ 1 oz FRESHLY GRATED
    PARMESAN CHEESE
SALT AND PEPPER

Wash the potatoes well, but leave their skins on.

Cook them in boiling salted water until tender. Drain and remove the skin. Press the hot potatoes through a fine metal sieve with the back of a spoon.

Stir in the oil, cream, olives and Parmesan and season to taste with salt and pepper. (Remember that Parmesan is quite salty, so go steady with the salt.)

ONION AND SUN-DRIED TOMATO GRAVY

What would Yorkshire puddings be without lashings of good hot gravy? This gravy is as hearty and flavoursome as any made from meat drippings, and makes an excellent sauce to pour over all sorts of food.

1 tbsp EXTRA VIRGIN OLIVE OIL
1 LARGE ONION, CHOPPED
55 g/ 2 oz SUN-DRIED TOMATOES IN
    OIL, DRAINED AND CHOPPED
575 ml/ 1 pt VEGETABLE STOCK
3 tbsp SINGLE CREAM
SALT AND PEPPER

Heat the oil over a moderate heat in a heavy-based pan which has a lid and cook the onion, stirring constantly, for 5–10 minutes, or until well browned but not burned.

Add the sun-dried tomatoes and stock. Bring to the boil, cover and simmer for 15 minutes.

Liquidize the contents of the pan in a blender or food processor. Return to the pan, season to taste and add the cream.

Reheat and pour into a gravy boat or serving jug.

CODDLED PEARS IN SPICED RUM SAUCE

These poached pears are very easy to prepare, but it is better if you start them the day before. For a special occasion, decorate the stem of each pear with a bow of baby ribbon, or garnish them with mint or lemon balm leaves, or edible flowers.

170 g/ 6 oz SUGAR

¼ tsp SALT

**PIECE OF CINNAMON STICK, ABOUT
    10 cm/ 4 in LONG**

4 WHOLE CLOVES

**¼ tsp ALLSPICE (WHOLE BERRIES
    IF POSSIBLE)**

**PIECE OF GINGER, ABOUT 1 cm/ ½ in
    ACROSS, PEELED AND SLICED**

**6 FIRM PEARS, PEELED BUT WITH
    STALKS LEFT ON**

100 ml/ 3½ fl oz RUM

**ICE-CREAM, YOGURT, FROMAGE
    FRAIS OR WHIPPED CREAM, TO
    SERVE (OPTIONAL)**

In a large saucepan which has a lid, put the sugar, salt and spices with 2.25 litres/ 4 pt water. Bring to the boil. Cover, turn down the heat and simmer for 15 minutes.

Put the pears in the saucepan, standing them upright in the syrup. Cook, covered, over a low to moderate heat, until the pears are quite tender. The exact cooking time will vary very much, according to the type and hardness of the pears, but will probably be something between 30 minutes and 1 hour. Do not worry if the pointed ends of the pears stick out above the syrup, as they do not need so much cooking and will cook in the steam.

Remove the pears from the syrup and stand them on a plate. Strain the syrup into a clean pan large enough to hold the pears snugly in one layer. Discard the spices and stir the rum into the syrup.

Return the pears to the syrup and leave until quite cold (preferably 4–8 hours for the flavours to develop fully). Transfer the pears to a plate and chill.

Place the saucepan of syrup over a high heat and boil rapidly to reduce it to 300 ml/ ½ pt. Allow to cool and then chill.

To serve: place each pear upright on a plate or in a shallow dish, pour over the syrup and add ice-cream, yogurt etc, if liked. Garnish as described above.

Coddled Pears in Spiced Rum Sauce

Through the Looking Glass

Not all is what it seems at first sight in this topsy-turvy menu: what was once an upside-down apple tart has been turned on its head once more to become a spectacular savoury first course; schnitzels exchange meat for layers of vegetables and cheese; in this Alice in Wonderland meal, even a simple fruit pudding has turned to drink!

'TARTE TATIN' OF CARAMELIZED
PINK ONIONS AND SUN-DRIED
TOMATOES

'SCHNITZELS' OF GRUYÈRE-
STUFFED AUBERGINE
MANGO AND CUCUMBER SALSA
SULTANA AND PINE KERNEL PILAF
WITH ROSEMARY

MELON IN GINGER WINE WITH
STEM GINGER

'TARTE TATIN' OF CARAMELIZED PINK ONIONS AND SUN-DRIED TOMATOES

The classic Tarte Tatin is an upside-down tart made from caramelized apples and puff pastry. This is my savoury version which tastes just as good as it looks. If you can't get pink onions, leeks work equally well.

Sun-dried tomatoes preserved in oil are available in jars from delicatessens and large supermarkets.

30 g/ 1 oz BUTTER
900 g/ 2 lb EVEN-SIZED PINK ONIONS, CUT
    ACROSS INTO 2 cm/ ¾ in SLICES
2 tbsp SUGAR
55 g/ 2 oz SUN-DRIED TOMATOES IN
    OIL, DRAINED AND COARSELY
    CHOPPED (SEE ABOVE)
225 g/ 8 oz FROZEN PUFF PASTRY,
    DEFROSTED
OLIVE OIL, FOR GREASING
SALAD LEAVES, TO GARNISH

Preheat the oven to 220C/425F/gas7.

Melt the butter in a frying pan or sauté pan large enough to accommodate the onion slices snugly in one layer. If you do not have a big enough pan, work in two batches.

Sprinkle half the sugar over the onions and season them with salt and pepper, then pour in enough cold water barely to cover the onions.

Bring to the boil and simmer, undisturbed, for about 30 minutes, or until the onions are tender and all the liquid has evaporated to leave a sticky glaze. Keep a careful eye on the pan towards the end of cooking time, as the onions could easily burn.

Liberally oil the bottom of a large flan tin or other suitable ovenproof receptacle (I use a paella pan with a 23 cm/9 in diameter base) and evenly sprinkle it with the remaining sugar. Scatter the pieces of sun-dried tomato on top of that.

Carefully arrange the onion slices in the prepared pan and season with salt and pepper.

Roll out the pastry thinly and cut a circle just a little larger than the size of the pan. Arrange this over the onions, tucking in the edges. Chill until required.

Bake for 20–30 minutes, or until the pastry is crisp and golden.

Turn out on a warmed serving plate and serve hot, cut in wedges, with a few salad leaves as garnish.

'SCHNITZELS' OF GRUYÈRE-STUFFED AUBERGINE

I love aubergine in all its guises. Like the mushroom, it has a succulent texture which can easily replace meat in a vegetarian menu. These 'meaty' sandwiches of vegetable and cheese combine a crispy golden exterior with a melting gooey centre – almost a vegetarian chicken Kiev.

4 MEDIUM AUBERGINES (ABOUT
    900 g/ 2 lb IN TOTAL)
115 g/ 4 oz GRUYÈRE OR
    EMMENTAL CHEESE, GRATED
2 EGGS, BEATEN
170 g/ 6 oz FINE WHITE
    BREADCRUMBS
SALT AND PEPPER
FLOUR, FOR COATING
EXTRA VIRGIN OLIVE OIL, FOR
    FRYING AND GREASING

Cut each aubergine across diagonally into 6 slices about 2 cm/ ¾ in thick. Sprinkle them with salt and leave for 1 hour in a colander over the sink. The salt will draw out some of the bitter juices. Rinse well and pat dry on tea towels.

Preheat the oven to 200C/400F/gas6 and grease 2 baking sheets with oil.

Arrange 12 slices on a work surface and divide the cheese between them, then place the remaining 12 slices on top of these to make 'sandwiches'.

Season some flour in a shallow bowl and put the eggs and the breadcrumbs into two other such bowls. Dip the sandwiches first in the seasoned flour, then in the egg and then in the crumbs, shaking off the excess each time.

Heat a little olive oil in a large frying pan. Working in manageable batches and adding a little more oil when necessary, fry the sandwiches for 2 minutes on each side, then transfer them to the greased baking sheets and bake for 20 minutes.

Serve immediately, with the salsa.

MANGO AND CUCUMBER SALSA

A salsa is really just an uncooked sauce or relish, but they seem to be appearing more and more on the menus of trendy restaurants. This one is really quick to make and incredibly versatile. It is particularly good with crisply fried foods.

½ CUCUMBER
1 LARGE RIPE MANGO, PEELED,
    STONED AND FINELY CHOPPED
1 SMALL MILD ONION, THINLY
    SLICED AND SEPARATED INTO
    RINGS
2 MEDIUM FRESH CHILLI PEPPERS
    (OR MORE TO TASTE), DESEEDED
    AND FINELY CHOPPED
JUICE OF 1 LIME OR LEMON
SALT

Using a swivel vegetable peeler, cut the cucumber into long thin slivers.

Put these strips in a colander, sprinkle them liberally with salt and leave to drain for 30 minutes. This will draw out the water and make them wilt.

Rinse well under cold running water, drain again and pat dry on a clean tea towel.

Transfer to a bowl and add all the remaining ingredients. Mix well and allow to chill for at least 2 hours, or preferably overnight, to allow the flavours to develop.

SULTANA AND PINE KERNEL PILAF WITH ROSEMARY

Many years ago I ate the most sublime pilaf in a small waterfront restaurant on the south coast of Turkey. It was studded with pine kernels – the first I had encountered – and seemed strongly perfumed with a pine-like flavour.

It was not until years later that I realized that the mysterious pine-like flavour came not from the pine kernels but from rosemary. This is my version of that dish.

2 tbsp EXTRA VIRGIN OLIVE OIL
1 LARGE ONION, CHOPPED
350 g/ 12 oz BASMATI RICE, RINSED
   AND DRIED
85 g/ 3 oz SULTANAS
85 g/ 3 oz PINE KERNELS
1 heaped tsp FINELY CHOPPED
   FRESH ROSEMARY OR ¾ tsp DRIED
1.1 litres/ 2 pt VEGETABLE STOCK
1 heaped tbsp CHOPPED PARSLEY
SALT AND PEPPER

Heat the oil over a moderate heat in a large heavy-based saucepan which has a lid and cook the onion, stirring occasionally, for about 5 minutes, or until soft and translucent.

Add the rice and continue to cook, stirring, for another 3–4 minutes, or until each grain is coated with oil. Add the sultanas, pine kernels, rosemary and stock. Stir well.

Bring to the boil and cook, uncovered and undisturbed, over a high heat for about 10 minutes.

When all the stock has boiled away and the surface of the rice is pitted with little holes, turn off the heat and place a tea towel or two layers of paper towels over the top of the pan. Cover with the lid and leave for 30 minutes, during which time the rice will continue to cook in its own steam.

Fork up the rice (which will now be perfectly cooked) and season if necessary (the stock may have seasoned the rice sufficiently).

Turn the pilaf into a warmed serving dish and sprinkle with the parsley to serve.

MELON IN GINGER WINE WITH STEM GINGER

It is an English tradition to serve a wedge of melon dusted with ground ginger as a first course of a formal dinner or lunch. Here, this luscious fruit appears at the other end of the menu, again partnered by ginger – this time in a rather more exotic guise.

For an even prettier effect, mix melons with differently coloured flesh, such as cantaloupe with water melon.

Green ginger wine is available from supermarkets and wine merchants. Stem ginger preserved in syrup is available in small jars from delicatessens and good supermarkets.

1 LARGE OR 2 SMALL MELONS,
   HALVED, PEELED AND DESEEDED
12 PIECES OF STEM GINGER IN
   SYRUP (SEE ABOVE), DRAINED
   AND CHOPPED
250 ml/ 8 fl oz GREEN GINGER WINE
   (SEE ABOVE)

Cut the melon flesh into bite-sized cubes and put them in an attractive serving dish (glass looks lovely) or divide them between 6 wine glasses. Scatter over the chopped stem ginger and pour over the wine.

Chill for at least 2 hours, or up to 12, before serving.

RIGHT: *Melon in Ginger Wine with Stem Ginger*

The Breadwinner

Sometimes a little lateral thinking is called for when it comes to dreaming up new ideas for vegetarian main courses. Here a classic nursery pudding takes on a new role, swapping sugar and spice for all things nice in a savoury way to become a mouthwatering garlic-perfumed centrepiece to this three-course menu.

RADISHES AND CORN WAFERS WITH THREE PÂTÉS

**SAVOURY BREAD AND BUTTER PUDDING
SEASONAL VEGETABLES**

FRESH FIGS WITH RUM AND MASCARPONE

RADISHES AND CORN WAFERS WITH THREE PÂTÉS

These crispy golden savoury biscuits are based on an old American recipe, and take only seconds to make. They are traditionally made with corn meal, a coarse flour made from maize, but this can vary in quality and in the amount of water it will absorb. For this reason I make mine with 'easy-cook' polenta, which is more readily available from delicatessens and is pretty much the same thing.

It is nice to serve these with a variety of pâtés, like the three recipes given in the Breads and Basics section (see pages 22–24), but just one would do. Alternatively, offer a selection of dips.

Makes about 12 wafers

30 g/ 1 oz MELTED BUTTER, PLUS
   MORE FOR GREASING
115 g/ 4 oz 'EASY-COOK' POLENTA
   (SEE ABOVE)
½ tsp SALT
¼ tsp CHILLI POWDER
350 ml/ 12 fl oz BOILING WATER
2 BUNCHES OF PINK RADISHES,
   TO SERVE
PÂTÉS OR DIPS,
   TO SERVE (SEE ABOVE)

Preheat the oven to 200C/400F/gas6 and grease 2 or 3 baking sheets with butter.

Put the polenta in a heatproof bowl with the salt and chilli powder. Pour over the boiling water and stir vigorously to avoid lumps forming, then stir in the butter. The resulting batter should be the consistency of thin cream. If it is too thick, stir in a little more cold water.

Pour tablespoonfuls of the batter on the prepared baking sheets and spread each out as thinly as possible to make circles. You will probably only get 4–5 easily on each baking sheet, so cook them in batches.

Bake for about 20 minutes, or until the edges just begin to turn brown and crispy. Transfer to a wire rack to allow them to cool. They will become crisp as they cool.

Serve with the radishes and pâtés or dips.

SAVOURY BREAD AND BUTTER PUDDING

A clever twist on an old favourite, this unusual main course is cheap, tasty and satisfying. Cooked chicory gives a particularly savoury and distinctive flavour to the creamy custard.

55 g/ 2 oz BUTTER, PLUS MORE FOR
   GREASING
115 g/ 4 oz CARROT, FINELY DICED
225 g/ 8 oz LEEK (ABOUT 1 LARGE
   LEEK), SLICED
225 g/ 8 oz CHICORY (ABOUT 2
   SMALL HEADS), SLICED
JUICE OF ½ LEMON
1 tbsp SUGAR
115 g/ 4 oz CIABATTA OR FRENCH
   BREAD, CUT INTO SLICES ABOUT
   6 mm/ ¼ in THICK
3 EGGS, LIGHTLY BEATEN
300 ml/ ½ pt MILK
300 ml/ ½ pt SINGLE CREAM
2 GARLIC CLOVES, CRUSHED
SALT AND PEPPER

Preheat the oven to 160C/325F/gas3 and grease a deep ovenproof dish with butter.

Melt half the butter over a moderate heat in a heavy-based saucepan which has a lid and stir-fry the carrot for 2 minutes.

Add the leek, chicory, lemon juice and sugar and season well with salt and pepper. Turn down the heat as low as possible, cover the pan and sweat the vegetables, stirring occasionally, for 10–15 minutes or until quite soft.

Spread the remaining butter on the slices of bread.

Arrange half these, buttered side up, in the bottom of the prepared dish. Arrange the cooked vegetables on top of the bread and butter and then cover with the remaining slices of bread, buttered side up.

Mix the eggs with the milk, cream and garlic and season with salt and pepper. Pour this over the contents of the dish and bake for 1¼–1½ hours, or until the custard is set and the top is crisp and golden.

LEFT: *Savoury Bread and Butter Pudding;*
RIGHT: *Fresh Figs with Rum and Mascarpone (page 85)*

FRESH FIGS WITH RUM AND MASCARPONE

I discovered this recipe in a tiny restaurant in the mountains of Liguria in North-west Italy, where I ate a splendid lunch outside one perfect day in late summer and the figs were still warm from the tree. Try this whenever you see fresh figs on sale – even better if you can pick them yourself when holidaying abroad!

**24 VERY RIPE LARGE FIGS
    PREFERABLY BLACK
6 tbsp (OR MORE) DARK RUM
6 tbsp (OR MORE) MASCARPONE
    CHEESE**

Cut a deep cross in the top of each fig and put 4 in each of 6 bowls.

Drizzle over the rum, blob on the mascarpone and serve.

Farmer's Basket

Imagine a small country market in a Mediterranean village . . . think of stalls groaning with fat ripe fruit and vegetables, sun-ripened, tight-skinned and bursting with goodness . . . and you have the first course of this menu.

A basket of the freshest of free-range eggs becomes the second course, and for the pudding we raid the orchards and meadows of northern France for apples, Calvados and rich fresh cream.

CAPONATA

GRATIN OF EGGS WITH SMOTHERED ONIONS AND ROQUEFORT
BASMATI RICE

APPLE TARTS WITH CALVADOS CREAM SAUCE

CAPONATA

I adore all kinds of Italian food, particularly the thousands of inventive and delicious ways in which they prepare and cook vegetables. A good example is this wonderful sweet-and-sour dish from the spectacularly beautiful island of Sicily. The only traditional ingredient which must be left out to make this a vegetarian dish is the anchovy, but there are so many other flavoursome ingredients that the loss is barely noticeable.

675 g/ 1½ lb AUBERGINE, CUT INTO
  2.5 cm/ 1 in CUBES
4 tbsp EXTRA VIRGIN OLIVE OIL
4 CELERY STALKS, CUT INTO 1 cm/
  ½ in LENGTHS
1 LARGE ONION, CHOPPED
3 tbsp SUGAR
5 tbsp RED WINE VINEGAR
400 g/ 14 oz CANNED ITALIAN
  PEELED TOMATOES, DRAINED
2 tbsp CONCENTRATED
  TOMATO PASTE
115 g/ 4 oz LARGE STONED
  GREEN OLIVES

2 tbsp SULTANAS
1½ tbsp CAPERS
30 g/ 1 oz PINE KERNELS
SALT AND PEPPER
CHOPPED FLAT-LEAF PARSLEY,
  TO GARNISH
LEMON WEDGES, TO SERVE

Place the aubergine cubes in a colander, sprinkle them generously with salt and leave for 1 hour to allow any bitter juices to be drawn out. Rinse well and dry thoroughly.

Caponata

the cooked vegetables to the pan.

Mix the sugar and vinegar and add this to the pan together with the tomatoes, tomato paste, olives, sultanas and capers. Season well with salt and pepper. Bring to the boil, reduce the heat and simmer, stirring frequently, for 15 minutes. Then add the pine kernels.

Transfer to a serving dish and allow to cool. Garnish with parsley and lemon wedges to serve.

GRATIN OF EGGS WITH SMOTHERED ONIONS AND ROQUEFORT

The success of this simple dish lies in the long slow cooking of the onions, as this renders them sweet and melting to contrast superbly with the strong sharp flavour of the cheese in the sauce.

You can make this in one big gratin dish, or 6 individual ones for a more formal presentation. For a special occasion, replace the more usual hens' eggs with quails' eggs which are now available from most large supermarkets and delicatessens.

3 tbsp EXTRA VIRGIN OLIVE OIL

900 g/ 2 lb ONIONS, SLICED

85 g/ 3 oz BUTTER, PLUS MORE
   FOR GREASING

9 LARGE HARD-BOILED EGGS,
   SHELLED AND HALVED, OR 36
   WHOLE HARD-BOILED QUAILS'
   EGGS (SEE ABOVE), SHELLED

55 g/ 2 oz FLOUR

575 ml/ 1 pt MILK

115 g/ 4 oz ROQUEFORT CHEESE,
   CRUMBLED

55 g/ 2 oz FRESH BREADCRUMBS,
   PREFERABLY WHITE

SALT AND PEPPER

Heat the oil over a moderate heat in a large heavy-based saucepan which has a lid and add the onions. Season with salt and pepper and cook, stirring, for 5–10 minutes, or until the onions just begin to soften.

Turn down the heat as low as possible and press a circle of greaseproof paper (or a butter paper) down on top of the onions. Put the lid on the pan and leave the onions to cook for about 1 hour, removing the paper and stirring the onions occasionally. (The paper holds in the steam, which helps the onions to cook without burning.) The cooked onions should be very soft and a rich golden brown.

Towards the end of the onion cooking time, preheat the oven to 180C/350F/ gas4 and grease a large ovenproof dish (or 6 individual ones) with butter.

Smooth the cooked onions over the bottom of the prepared dish(es) and arrange the eggs on top of that.

Melt two-thirds of the butter in a clean saucepan and add the flour. Cook this roux over a moderate heat for 2–3 minutes, stirring constantly. Add the milk and bring to the boil, stirring constantly (I use a balloon whisk for this job). When the sauce thickens, turn down the heat and simmer for about 5 minutes. Then add the cheese and season the sauce with salt and pepper. Cook, stirring, for 2–3 minutes more, or just until the cheese has melted and the sauce is smooth.

Pour the sauce over the eggs, then sprinkle with the breadcrumbs and dot with the remaining butter, cut into small pieces.

Bake for about 30 minutes or until crisp, golden and bubbling. Serve with plain boiled or steamed Basmati rice.

Heat half the oil in a large frying pan (I use a wok) over a moderate heat and stir-fry the celery for 10 minutes. Add the onion and continue to cook, stirring frequently, for another 10 minutes, or until the onion is soft and golden.

Remove the cooked vegetables from the pan with a slotted spoon and transfer them to a bowl.

Heat the remaining oil in the pan and cook the dried aubergine cubes over a moderate heat, stirring frequently, for 8–10 minutes or until golden. Return

APPLE TARTS WITH CALVADOS CREAM SAUCE

This wonderful variation on a classic recipe from Normandy was given to me by chef Jean-Pierre Lelettier of the Hôtel de France at des Fuchsias.

Of course, Jean-Pierre made his own puff pastry – and you can if you are good at it – but it is much simpler to buy the frozen type available in many large supermarkets which comes already rolled out in separate sheets.

Calvados, the apple brandy from Normandy, is available from most large supermarkets and good wine merchants.

6 SHEETS OF READY-ROLLED PUFF PASTRY (SEE ABOVE)
6 EATING APPLES
4 tbsp SIEVED APRICOT JAM
For the sauce
85 g/ 3 oz SUGAR
300 ml/ ½ pt SINGLE CREAM
2 tbsp CALVADOS OR BRANDY
For the purée
3 EATING APPLES, PEELED, CORED AND CHOPPED
30 g/ 1 oz BUTTER

First make the sauce: put the sugar in a small pan with just enough water to dissolve it. Cook over a moderate heat, without stirring, until a golden caramel is formed.

Pour in all the cream at once. The caramel will solidify. Bring to the boil. Then turn down the heat and simmer, stirring constantly, for 2–3 minutes, until all the caramel is dissolved. Remove from the heat and add the Calvados or brandy. Chill.

Preheat the oven to 200C/400F/gas6.

Cut six 15 cm/6 in circles from the pastry and arrange these on a dampened baking sheet. Chill until required.

Make the purée: peel, core and chop the apples, then cook them with 2 tablespoons of water and the butter over a very low heat for about 10–15 minutes, or until mushy. Purée in a blender or food processor or mash with a potato masher. Allow to cool.

Place the apple halves, cut side down, on a chopping board in front of you. The cavity from which the core came should be running away from you. Starting at the right-hand side (left if you are left-handed), with a knife blade pointing away from you, slice the apple as thinly as possible, gradually angling the tip of the knife to the left (or right, if left-handed) as you slice. The cuts should end up in a slight fan shape. Push the sliced apple half over like a pack of cards and it will fan out to make a perfect semi-circle.

Put a tablespoon of the purée on each pastry circle, spreading it evenly but leaving a clear 2.5 cm/1 in border all the way round. Arrange two semi-circles of apple slices over the purée. This should cover the purée completely and make a full circle.

Bake for about 20 minutes, or until the apple is tender and the pastry border is golden brown.

Towards the end of this time, melt the jam in a small pan with 2 tablespoons of water. As soon as the tarts come out of the oven, brush them all over with the mixture to glaze.

To serve, pour the chilled sauce on 6 large plates and place a warm tart on top. Serve immediately.

Apple Tart with Calvados Cream Sauce

The Colours of Summer

Food should not only smell and taste appetizing, but look good! Nothing could look more gorgeous than this colourful procession of delicious dishes — crimson tomatoes, golden polenta, a brilliant salad of primary colours and the jewel-like hues of glistening summer fruits — in a menu to delight both the eye and the palate.

TOMATO AND BASIL SALAD
ROSEMARY FOCACCIA

GRILLED POLENTA WITH MUSHROOMS, ARTICHOKES AND BRIE
GREEN AND ORANGE SALAD

SUMMER FRUIT SALAD IN PINEAU DES CHARENTES

TOMATO AND BASIL SALAD

Surely there can be few more perfect combinations of flavour than tomato and basil, and what could be better – or easier – to start a summer meal than this classic salad.

It does, however, rely on superb ripe tomatoes. Our supermarkets have at last started to grow tomatoes 'for flavour', but if you can only find Dutch hothouse tomatoes, don't bother.

The sun-dried tomatoes in this recipe are far from classic, but give the salad a bit of 'bite' and emphasize the tomato flavour.

900 g/ 2 lb RIPE TOMATOES (SEE
    ABOVE), SLICED
4 tbsp VINAIGRETTE (SEE PAGE 18)
1 GARLIC CLOVE, CRUSHED
2 tbsp SUN-DRIED TOMATOES IN OIL,
    DRAINED AND CHOPPED
    (OPTIONAL – SEE ABOVE)
2 tbsp (OR MORE) FRESH
    BASIL LEAVES

Arrange the tomato slices on a serving plate or in a shallow dish.

Mix the garlic into the vinaigrette and drizzle this over the tomatoes. Sprinkle with the sun-dried tomatoes, if using, and leave for 30 minutes to 1 hour at room temperature to allow the flavours to develop fully.

Sprinkle with the basil just before serving.

ROSEMARY FOCACCIA

This flat Italian bread is really a very simple pizza. There are almost as many variations on the recipe as there are cooks in Italy. My simple version uses dried 'easy-blend' yeast, which is added to the dry ingredients and is much easier and quicker to use than the traditional kind. It is available from most supermarkets and grocers.

675 g/ 1½ lb STRONG
  WHITE FLOUR
1 sachet (1 tbsp)
  'EASY-BLEND' YEAST
1½ tsp SALT
2 tbsp FRESH ROSEMARY OR
  1½ tbsp DRIED
3 tbsp EXTRA VIRGIN OLIVE OIL,
  PLUS MORE FOR GREASING
450 ml/ ¾ pt HAND-HOT WATER
ROCK SALT

Place the flour in a large bowl with the yeast and salt and half the rosemary. Stir in 2 tablespoons of the oil and the hot water and bring the mixture together to form a ball of dough.

Knead the dough for a good 10 minutes as described on page 15.

Form the dough into an even ball and place it on a floured board. Sprinkle the top with flour and cover with floured film or a floured lightweight cloth and leave it in a warm place (not too warm – just an average kitchen will do) to rise, until about doubled in size (see page 15).

Preheat the oven to 230C/450F/gas8 and lightly grease a 37.5 × 27.5 cm/ 15 × 10¾ in baking sheet with a little oil.

Roll out the dough on the prepared baking sheet and leave it to rise again for about 1 hour, until the dough has doubled in thickness.

With the fingertips, make indentations all over the surface of the dough. Then drizzle over the remaining olive oil or paint it on with a brush. Sprinkle over the remaining rosemary and a liberal sprinkling of rock salt.

Bake for about 15 minutes, or until golden and cooked through. Cut into rectangles and serve warm or cold.

GRILLED POLENTA WITH MUSHROOMS, ARTICHOKES AND BRIE

Polenta is a kind of porridge made from a coarse flour ground from maize, and is much loved by the Italians who eat it in all kinds of different ways. In this recipe it is left to go cold and set into a kind of loaf, then sliced and grilled or fried until crispy.

Originally polenta had to be stirred constantly on the top of a stove for a very long time, but now 'easy-cook' polenta needs only a fraction of the cooking time and is readily available from good delicatessens.

1.5 litres/ 2½ pt VEGETABLE STOCK
1 tsp SALT
375 g/ 13 oz 'EASY-COOK' POLENTA
  (SEE ABOVE)
5 tbsp EXTRA VIRGIN OLIVE OIL,
  PLUS MORE FOR GREASING
350 g/ 12 oz MUSHROOMS, SLICED
2 GARLIC CLOVES, CRUSHED
2 tbsp CHOPPED PARSLEY
225 g/ 8 oz CANNED ARTICHOKE
  BOTTOMS, DRAINED AND
  THINLY SLICED
450 g/ 1 lb BRIE, CUT VERTICALLY
  INTO THIN SLICES (INCLUDING
  THE RIND)
SALT AND PEPPER

Add the salt to the stock and bring it to the boil in a saucepan. Then add the polenta in a slow steady stream, stirring very thoroughly to prevent lumps forming. Simmer, stirring, for 5–10 minutes.

Pour into an oiled 1.75 litre/3 pt loaf tin and leave for at least 1 hour to cool and set.

Preheat a hot grill if using.

Turn the polenta out on a chopping board and cut off 12 slices about 1 cm/½ in thick (save the rest for another day).

Using about 3 tablespoons in all, brush the slices on both sides with the olive oil. Working in manageable batches, either grill or fry the polenta slices (I use a heavy 'le Creuset' ridged frying pan which produces attractive 'grilled' stripes) for about 3–4 minutes on each side, until golden and crispy. Keep these warm while you cook the rest.

Meanwhile, heat the remaining oil in a frying pan or wok over a moderate heat and stir-fry the mushrooms with the garlic and parsley for 5–10 minutes, until completely softened. Stir in the artichoke slices, season with salt and pepper and cook for 1 minute more.

Preheat the oven to 190C/375F/gas5 and grease a baking sheet with oil.

Arrange 6 of the polenta slices on the prepared baking sheet and divide the mushroom mixture between them, piling it high and trying to keep it within the confines of the slices. Top with the other polenta slices so that you have 6 'sandwiches'. Pile the cheese slices on top of these and bake for about 5 minutes, or until the cheese has melted.

Serve immediately with the salad.

GREEN AND ORANGE SALAD

*Carrot is not often used in mixed salads.
However, grated and combined with lettuce
leaves it adds a nice sweet crunchiness and
a fabulous splash of colour to the meal
table.*

*If it is the nasturtium season (many
supermarkets now sell them in the salad
section) they will add more jolly colour and
an interesting slightly bitter tang.*

115 g/ 4 oz GREEN SALAD LEAVES,
   TORN INTO SMALLISH PIECES
2 SMALL CARROTS OR
   1 LARGE, GRATED
4 tbsp VINAIGRETTE (SEE PAGE 18)
NASTURTIUM FLOWERS, TO
   GARNISH (OPTIONAL)

Mix the leaves and grated carrot in a
salad bowl.

Just before serving, toss with the
vinaigrette dressing and scatter over the
nasturtiums, if using.

SUMMER FRUIT SALAD IN PINEAU DES CHARENTES

Pineau des Charentes is a delicious French aperitif wine made in Cognac from a combination of grape juice and brandy. The white version is fruity and grape-like and best served chilled or with ice as an aperitif. The rosé version, which is deep red and rather port-like, is best served at the end of a meal and is particularly good with cheese.

Although incredibly popular in France, until recently Pineau was hardly known in this country. Luckily it is now available from some supermarkets and good wine merchants. Not only is it good to drink, it is excellent to use in recipes, both sweet and savoury (see also the Passion Fruit and Pineau Syllabub on page 101).

675–900 g/ 1½–2 lb SUMMER FRUIT, CUT INTO BITE-SIZED PIECES
300 ml/ ½ pt WHITE PINEAU DES CHARENTES (SEE ABOVE)
SUGAR, FOR FROSTING

Put the fruit in a bowl with the Pineau and mix well. Cover with film and chill for 3–6 hours to allow the flavours to develop.

Frost the rims of 6 large wine glasses by dipping them first in water and then in sugar.

Divide the fruit between the decorated glasses, making sure everyone gets a good share of 'juice', and serve immediately.

Pizza Party

This is a wonderful menu for the sort of informal occasion when family and friends gather with a drink around the barbecue or gossip in the kitchen (they can then help with the pizza topping). It makes a perfect summer party for the young, old and the rest of us.

BARBECUED VEGETABLE PLATTER

PIZZA OF RADICCHIO, CHÈVRES, TOMATOES, OLIVES AND CAPERS

PASSION FRUIT AND PINEAU SYLLABUB WITH BURNT SUGAR SHARDS

BARBECUED VEGETABLE PLATTER

Barbecues are usually associated with meat, but why should vegetarians miss out on the fun? Lots of vegetables are delicious grilled over glowing charcoal!

The list of vegetables below is just intended as a guideline: try your own combinations and add or substitute peppers and aubergines (prepared as on pages 24 and 124 respectively) or whole tomatoes and courgettes cut across at an angle.

In bad weather, or if you don't own a barbecue, simply use the grill in the kitchen.

2 SMALL FENNEL BULBS, HARD
   CORES REMOVED
3 SMALL CHICORY HEADS
2 SMALL TIGHT HEADS OF
   RADICCHIO, TRIMMED OF ANY
   TATTY, LOOSE OUTSIDE LEAVES
150 ml/ ¼ pt EXTRA VIRGIN
   OLIVE OIL
SALT AND PEPPER
LEMON WEDGES, TO SERVE
SPRIGS OF FRESH HERBS,
   TO GARNISH

Cut the fennel bulbs from top to bottom into 6 slices about 1 cm/½ in thick. Cut each head of chicory lengthwise into 4 long wedges, removing most of the hard core, but leaving enough to hold the leaves together. Cut the radicchio heads from top to bottom into 6 slices about 1 cm/½ in thick. Any leftover bits of the vegetables can be kept for salad.

Brush the vegetable slices thoroughly all over with olive oil, sprinkle with salt and pepper and leave on a plate to marinate for about 30 minutes.

Preheat a hot barbecue or very hot grill.

Brush the vegetable slices with oil once more. Working in manageable batches, arrange them over the hot barbecue, or on a foil-lined grill pan. Cook for about 3–4 minutes, turning once, or until hot and softened with the edges just beginning to blacken. Remove from the barbecue or grill and keep warm while you cook the rest.

Arrange the cooked vegetables on a large warmed platter and garnish with fresh herbs and lemon wedges. Serve with good crusty bread.

PIZZA OF RADICCHIO, CHÈVRES, TOMATOES, OLIVES AND CAPERS

I wasn't a great pizza fan until I bought my house in the South of France. In our village there is a small restaurant which specializes in pizzas, salads and puddings. The pizzas are cooked in a wood-fired oven and have the thinnest of crusts. I also learnt that pizza toppings don't have to include tomato sauce! Suffice it to say that when I am in London I dream of those pizzas. This is my attempt to copy them and, although I only have a normal domestic oven in which to cook them, I am very pleased with the result.

On one occasion, when I couldn't get chèvre (goats' cheese), I made this recipe with Feta and it was just as good. Unless you happen to have an enormous oven, the most you will be able to cook is 2 pizzas at a time, so your guests will have to share out these as you cook them – or be patient.

6 tbsp EXTRA VIRGIN OLIVE OIL,
    PLUS MORE FOR GREASING
1 QUANTITY WHITE HOMEMADE
    BREAD DOUGH (SEE PAGE 15),
    LEFT TO RISE
3 SMALL FIRM RADICCHIO HEARTS
    (USE THE OUTER LEAVES FOR
    SALAD)
1.35 k/ 3 lb REALLY RIPE TOMATOES,
    SLICED
2 MILD ONIONS, THINLY SLICED
350 g/ 12 oz FRESH GOATS' CHEESE
    (SEE ABOVE), CUT INTO SMALL
    CUBES
36 STONED OLIVES (BLACK OR
    GREEN, OR MIXED)
2 tbsp CAPERS, DRAINED
SALT AND PEPPER

Preheat the oven to 230C/450F/gas8 and grease 2 or 3 baking sheets with oil.

Divide the dough into 6 equal parts and roll these out on a floured surface to make very thin discs about 25 cm/10 in across. Arrange these on the baking sheets.

Divide the radicchio, tomatoes, onions, cheese, olives and capers between the pizza bases and drizzle 1 tablespoon of olive oil over each.

Season with salt and pepper and bake for 15 minutes (see above), or until the pizza bases are crisp.

PASSION FRUIT AND PINEAU SYLLABUB WITH BURNT SUGAR SHARDS

A variation on the the great classic British recipe, I love this recipe not just because it tastes so wonderful, but because it takes only a few minutes to make.

The sugar shards aren't exactly necessary, but the spectacular result is way out of proportion to the little effort it takes to produce them. Passion fruit are now readily available in large supermarkets.

150 ml/ ¼ pt PINEAU DES
    CHARENTES (SEE PAGE 97)
    OR SHERRY
PULP FROM 8 PASSION FRUIT
85 g/ 3 oz GRANULATED SUGAR
300 ml/ ½ pt DOUBLE CREAM

Place the Pineau, 55 g/2 oz of the sugar and the cream in a bowl and whisk until the mixture forms soft peaks. Whisk in half the passion fruit pulp.

Pour into 6 wine glasses and chill until required.

Make the sugar shards: preheat a hot grill. Cover a baking sheet with foil, making sure it is absolutely smooth. Sprinkle over just enough of the remaining granulated sugar just to cover it, but leaving a good border uncovered around the edge.

Place the baking sheet under the hot grill, arranging it as far away from the heat as possible. In 2–3 minutes, the sugar will dissolve into a golden liquid caramel. Remove the sheet from the grill and allow to cool. The caramel will become hard and brittle, like glass. Peel away the foil and break the caramel into 'shards'.

Just before serving, spoon the remaining passion fruit pulp over the syllabubs and spear them with the sugar shards. Serve immediately.

Three Star Meal

A substantial main course, with accompanying vegetables and sauces, takes centre stage in most meals, with the first and last courses playing minor roles. In this elegant menu for a special occasion, however, three mouthwatering sophisticated little dishes vie for attention in successive cameo parts.

ASPARAGUS MOUSSES WITH VEGETABLE BEURRE BLANC

**GNOCCHI WITH SPINACH AND PEAS
GREEN SALAD**

AUSTRALIAN APPLE CHOCOLATE CAKE

ASPARAGUS MOUSSES WITH VEGETABLE BEURRE BLANC

Although these lovely little moulds of creamy asparagus custard are very easy to make, they are absolutely spectacular and taste as wonderful as anything you might be served in the poshest of French restaurants.

The sauce will keep warm for up to 30 minutes, if left standing in a pan or bowl of hot water.

30 g/ 1 oz BUTTER, PLUS MORE
   FOR GREASING
450 g/ 1 lb ASPARAGUS STALKS,
   BOTTOM THIRD TRIMMED OFF
1 SMALL ONION, CHOPPED
3 EGGS
125 ml/ 4 fl oz DOUBLE CREAM
SALT AND PEPPER
For the vegetable beurre
   blanc sauce
2 SHALLOTS, FINELY CHOPPED
3 tbsp WHITE WINE
3 tbsp WHITE WINE VINEGAR
225 g/ 8 oz CHILLED UNSALTED
   BUTTER, CUT INTO 2.5 cm/ 1 in
   CUBES
55 g/ 2 oz COOKED BROAD BEANS
55 g/ 2 oz COOKED DICED CARROT

Preheat the oven to 190C/375F/gas5 and grease 6 small ovenproof moulds with butter.

Cook the asparagus in boiling salted water for 8–10 minutes, or until tender. Drain, refresh in cold water and drain again. Reserve 12 tips for the sauce.

Melt the butter in a small heavy-based saucepan and cook the onion over a medium heat, stirring occasionally, until softened.

Whizz the asparagus and onion in a blender or food processor until puréed. With the machine still running, gradually add the eggs, followed by the cream. Season with salt and pepper.

Pour the mixture into the prepared moulds and cover the top of each with foil. Stand in a bain-marie, or a deep roasting tin half-filled with hot water, and bake for 35–40 minutes, or until firm.

Meanwhile make the sauce: place the shallots, wine and vinegar in a small saucepan and simmer over a low heat until reduced to about 2 tablespoons. This will take about 5 minutes, but must be done slowly so as to cook the shallot and allow it to give off its flavour.

Over a low to moderate heat, whisk in the chilled butter two pieces at a time, adding more as soon as they have melted. (It should take 3–4 minutes to incorporate all the butter.) If the sauce begins to bubble at any time, remove the pan from the heat for a moment as the butter will become oily if it becomes too hot. The finished sauce should be pale, creamy and emulsified. Season to taste with salt and pepper.

Add the cooked vegetables to the sauce and leave for 1 or 2 minutes to warm them through. Keep warm, if necessary (see above).

To serve: unmould the mousses on 6 warmed plates, pour the vegetable sauce around them and serve at once.

GNOCCHI WITH SPINACH AND PEAS

These semolina gnocchi are a variation on gnocchi alla romana, layered with spinach and peas and crusted with bubbling Parmesan. Serve them piping hot, straight from the oven.

The gnocchi can be made several hours ahead of time and simply popped in the oven at the last minute. Buy the semolina from an Italian delicatessen, if possible.

500 g/ 1 lb 2 oz FRESH SPINACH
85 g/ 3 oz BUTTER
1 litre/ 1¾ pt MILK
200 g/ 7 oz SEMOLINA
85 g/ 3 oz FRESHLY GRATED
   PARMESAN CHEESE
2 EGGS, LIGHTLY BEATEN
170 g/ 6 oz FROZEN PETITS POIS,
   DEFROSTED
SALT AND PEPPER
FRESHLY GRATED NUTMEG

Wash the spinach and dry it thoroughly, preferably by spinning it in a salad spinner.

Melt one-third of the butter over a moderate heat in a heavy-based saucepan which has a lid. Add the spinach, cover and cook, shaking the pan occasionally, for about 3 minutes, or until the spinach has just wilted. Season it with salt and pepper and a pinch of nutmeg, then leave to drain in a colander.

Bring the milk to the boil in a large saucepan with half the remaining butter. Pour in the semolina in a steady stream, stirring constantly to avoid lumps forming. Turn down the heat as low as possible and season with salt and pepper and a pinch of nutmeg. Simmer for 10 minutes, stirring frequently (this is most easily done with a hand-held electric rotary whisk), then stir in half of the Parmesan. Remove from the heat, allow to cool for 1–2 minutes, then beat in the eggs.

With a wetted spatula or large knife and working quickly, spread the mixture on a wetted smooth surface (either marble or Formica) to form an even layer about 1 cm/½ in thick. Leave to cool completely (about 1 hour).

Preheat the oven to 220C/425F/gas7.

Using a wetted 5 cm/2 in pastry cutter or rim of a small glass, punch out circles from the sheet. Scatter the 'trimmings' (the little bits between the circles) over the bottom of a greased baking dish.

Spread the cooked spinach over this, followed by the peas. Working carefully as they are fragile, arrange the gnocchi circles over the top, slightly overlapping them like roof tiles.

Sprinkle over the remaining cheese and dot with the remaining butter. Bake for 15–20 minutes, or until golden and bubbling.

Serve with a green salad.

AUSTRALIAN APPLE CHOCOLATE CAKE

Sydney is undoubtedly my favourite city, not just for the weather and the beaches but for all the wonderful restaurants the city boasts. A rising young chef in this restaurant scene, Dov Soconi, gave me the recipe for this stunning cake, which is light and moist and contains no fat or flour. It is also incredibly quick and easy. Serve it just as it is, dusted with icing sugar or with whipped cream and fresh fruit.

4 EGGS, SEPARATED
115 g/ 4 oz SUGAR
115 g/ 4 oz PLAIN CHOCOLATE,
   MELTED
1 DESSERT APPLE, PEELED, CORED
   AND GRATED
115 g/ 4 oz GROUND ALMONDS
VEGETABLE OIL, FOR GREASING

Preheat the oven to 180C/350F/gas4 and oil a 20 cm/8 in loose-bottomed cake tin.

Beat the egg yolks with the sugar until light and fluffy, then mix in the sugar, chocolate, apple and almonds.

Beat the egg whites until stiff and fold them into the mixture.

Pour it into the prepared cake tin and bake for about 45 minutes, or until a skewer inserted into the cake comes out clean.

Remove the cake from the tin and leave to cool on a wire rack.

New World Warmer

Chase away the chills of winter by indulging in this spicy and comforting menu with more than a hint of influence from the Americas – from Mexico to New England!

REFRIED BEANS WITH MELTED CHEESE AND AVOCADO

CHILLI CON FUNGHI AND SPOON BREAD PIE
WILTED WATERCRESS WITH OLIVE OIL AND GARLIC

NEW ENGLAND APPLE SHORTCAKES

REFRIED BEANS WITH MELTED CHEESE AND AVOCADO

Although far from authentic, this recipe is based on a traditional Mexican dish and makes an unusual first course. To serve it as a light lunch or supper dish, add a rather more substantial salad.

Chilli peppers vary enormously in 'hotness', and how much you should add is very much a matter of personal taste – and endurance! In general, the larger they are the milder they are; so, in fact, one big one would have roughly the same effect as one small one in the amount of fieriness it would add to a dish.

6 tbsp OLIVE OIL

2 LARGE ONIONS, CHOPPED

2 GARLIC CLOVES, CRUSHED

2 CHILLI PEPPERS, DESEEDED AND
  FINELY CHOPPED (SEE ABOVE)

800 g/ 1 lb CANNED RED KIDNEY
  BEANS, DRAINED

170 g/ 6 oz FARMHOUSE CHEDDAR
  CHEESE, GRATED

3 LARGE RIPE AVOCADOS

JUICE OF 2 LIMES

SALT AND PEPPER

To garnish

SALAD LEAVES

LIME WEDGES

SLICED DESEEDED CHILLI PEPPER
  (OPTIONAL)

Heat two-thirds of the oil in a frying pan over a low to moderate heat and cook the onions with the garlic and chilli peppers, stirring occasionally, for 10–15 minutes or until soft and brown.

Either mash the beans with a fork or whizz them briefly in a blender or food processor and add the resulting coarse purée to the contents of the pan. Mix well and season generously with salt and pepper. Transfer the mixture to a bowl and chill.

Form the chilled mixture into 12 burger-shaped patties, about 1 cm/½ in thick.

Heat the remaining oil in the frying pan and fry the patties, in manageable batches, for 2–3 minutes on each side. Keep them warm while cooking the remainder.

Towards the end of this cooking, pre-heat a hot grill. Arrange the cooked patties in the grill pan, sprinkle with the cheese and grill until the cheese melts.

Meanwhile, peel, stone and slice the avocados. Toss the slices lightly in the lime juice.

Arrange 2 patties on each plate, surrounded by the dressed avocado slices and garnish them with the salad leaves, lime wedges and chilli slices, if using.

CHILLI CON FUNGHI AND SPOON BREAD PIE

This recipe is adapted from one I found in an old American recipe book. The original 'chilli' pie filling was 'con carne' (made with minced beef), but chopped fresh meaty mushrooms make a perfect substitute and the finished dish is much lighter and fresher tasting. However, a few dried mushrooms add a wonderful rich earthy flavour. Use either Chinese dried mushrooms, which are available from oriental stores, or Italian funghi porcini, which are available from most delicatessens.

Spoon bread is an American dish which is a cross between corn bread and a soufflé. The corn meal for the spoon bread is available from delicatessens and some large supermarkets. If it is not readily available substitute Italian 'easy-cook' polenta, which may be found in most delicatessens.

15 g/ ½ oz DRIED MUSHROOMS
  (SEE ABOVE)

2 tbsp OLIVE OIL

2 ONIONS, CHOPPED

450 g/ 1 lb MUSHROOMS, COARSELY
  CHOPPED

1 GREEN SWEET PEPPER,
  DESEEDED AND COARSELY
  CHOPPED

450 g/ 1 lb CANNED TOMATOES

4–6 (DEPENDING ON TASTE) FRESH
  CHILLI PEPPERS, DESEEDED AND
  FINELY CHOPPED

450 g/ 1 lb CANNED RED KIDNEY
  BEANS, DRAINED

CHILLI POWDER (OPTIONAL)

SALT AND PEPPER

For the spoon bread topping

500 ml/ 16 fl oz MILK

3 EGGS

30 g/ 1 oz UNSALTED BUTTER

85 g/ 3 oz CORN MEAL (SEE ABOVE)

½ tsp SALT

1½ tsp BAKING POWDER

Soak the dried mushrooms for 30 minutes in 100 ml/3½ fl oz hot water. Then drain them well, straining and reserving the soaking liquid, and chop the soaked mushrooms coarsely.

Heat the olive oil in a saucepan over a moderate heat and fry the onions for 5–10 minutes, stirring frequently, until they are soft and translucent. Add the fresh mushrooms and continue to cook, stirring occasionally, for another 5 minutes or until the mushrooms begin to soften.

Add the chopped dried mushrooms and their soaking liquid, the chopped sweet pepper, the tomatoes with their liquid, the chilli peppers and beans. Season with salt and pepper. Cook over a moderate heat for about 15 minutes, stirring occasionally. The sauce should quite be thick, rather like Bolognese sauce. If it is too runny, turn up the heat and cook a little longer to evaporate off some of the liquid.

Check the seasoning at this stage. If you think you would like a little more 'fire', stir in a little chilli powder. Pour the sauce into a deep ovenproof dish and allow it to cool completely.

Preheat the oven to 200C/400F/gas6.

Make the spoon bread: whisk 125 ml/ 4 fl oz of the milk with the eggs in a bowl. In a medium saucepan, heat the remaining milk with the butter until it melts. When the mixture comes to the boil, turn down the heat as low as possible and sprinkle in the corn meal, whisking hard to make sure no lumps form. Add the salt and remove from the heat. Leave for 1–2 minutes to cool a little.

Gradually whisk the egg mixture into the cornmeal mixture until smooth. Beat in the baking powder and then pour the batter over the mushroom mixture. Bake for 30–40 minutes, until the spoon bread is well risen and golden brown.

WILTED WATERCRESS WITH OLIVE OIL AND GARLIC

Watercress is one of my favourite salad ingredients – I love its strong peppery flavour and attractive dark green leaves. Cooked, it is also an excellent vegetable accompaniment which makes a pleasant change from spinach. There is a traditional French recipe for cooking it with cream, but I prefer this combination with olive oil and garlic.

3 tbsp EXTRA VIRGIN OLIVE OIL
3 BUNCHES OF WATERCRESS,
    WASHED AND THOROUGHLY
    DRAINED (I USE A SALAD SPINNER)
2–3 GARLIC CLOVES (DEPENDING
    ON SIZE), CRUSHED
SQUEEZE OF LEMON JUICE
30 g/ 1 oz TOASTED FLAKED
    ALMONDS
SALT AND PEPPER

Heat the oil over a moderate to high heat in a heavy-based pan which has a lid. Put in the watercress, garlic, salt and pepper. Cover and cook for 1 minute. Stir well, replace the lid and cook for 2 minutes more.

Stir again, replace the lid, remove from the heat and leave the watercress to cook in its own steam for 2 more minutes.

Tip the contents of the pan into a warmed serving dish and sprinkle with the lemon juice and toasted almonds.

Serve at once.

NEW ENGLAND APPLE SHORTCAKES

In the USA, the term shortcake refers to something very like our scone. The most famous and best-loved version is strawberry shortcake, in which the freshly baked well-risen shortcake is split and filled with fresh strawberries and whipped cream, with perhaps more fruit and cream piled on top. This more wintry version is filled with spicy apples.

These are good served hot, warm or cold, but the shortcakes are best as freshly baked as possible.

Makes 8
For the filling
½ tsp SALT
PIECE OF CINNAMON STICK ABOUT
    10 cm/ 4 in LONG, BROKEN IN
    2 PIECES
2 SLICES OF LEMON
225 g/ 8 oz SUGAR
6 DESSERT APPLES, PEELED, CORED
    AND SLICED LENGTHWISE
For the shortcakes
55 g/ 2 oz BUTTER, PLUS MORE
    FOR GREASING
285 g/ 10 oz FLOUR
1 tsp SALT
2 tsp BAKING POWDER
1 heaped tbsp SUGAR
165 ml/ 5½ fl oz MILK
To serve
150 ml/ ¼ pt DOUBLE CREAM
1 tbsp SUGAR
¼ tsp VANILLA ESSENCE

First make the filling: put the salt, cinnamon, lemon slices and sugar in a pan together with 575 ml/1 pt water. Bring to the boil, add the apple slices and simmer for 5–10 minutes, or until the apple is tender but the slices still hold their shape.

Using a slotted spoon, remove the apples from the pan and reserve. Boil the liquid in the pan hard, until reduced to a syrup. Return the apples to the pan.

Make the shortcakes: preheat the oven to 230C/450F/gas8 and grease a baking tray with butter.

Sift the flour, salt, baking powder and sugar into a bowl. Then cut in the butter until the mixture resembles fine bread-crumbs. With a fork, mix in the milk and bring the mixture together to form a soft dough. (All this can be done in seconds in a food processor.)

Knead on a lightly floured surface for about 20 seconds, then pat out to a thickness of 1 cm/½ in. Using a 7.5 cm/3 in cutter, stamp out 8 rounds, re-rolling the trimmings as necessary. Place the rounds on the prepared baking tray and bake for 12 minutes.

Allow the shortcakes to cool, or serve them hot or warm. If serving hot, reheat the apple filling. Whip the cream with the sugar and vanilla to stiff peaks.

Split the shortcakes across their 'equator' and place a 'bottom' on each plate. Spoon over some apple slices with some syrup, followed by some of the whipped cream. Replace the 'lids' and spoon over more apples with syrup and then more cream, piling it as high as possible.

New England Apple Shortcake

Frozen Assets

Every child – from the age of 8 to 80 – loves ice-cream. The iced dessert that ends this rustic menu, however, is a particularly grown-up version, served in a way that will bring a smile of surprise to your guests' faces when they realize that the meal hasn't ended quite as abruptly as they thought!

GRILLED GOATS' CHEESE ON CORN BREAD WITH MUSHROOM RAGOUT

AVOCADO AND WALNUT RISOTTO VERY GREEN SALAD WITH HERB VINAIGRETTE

CAPPUCCINO ICE-CREAM

GRILLED GOATS' CHEESE ON CORN BREAD WITH MUSHROOM RAGOUT

I have only ever once entertained a professional chef to dinner – a nerve-racking experience! This was the first course I invented for that occasion. Luckily it was a huge success, and the rest of the evening went like a dream.

The corn bread and the mushroom mixture may be made in advance – the day before if you like – making this a quick and easy starter for those special occasions when you want to spend as much time as possible with your guests.

Either use fresh soft individual goats' cheeses, which are available from good cheese shops, or slices about 1 cm/ ½ in thick from the kind of chèvres sold in log shapes by most delicatessens.

15 g/ ½ oz DRIED MUSHROOMS
   (SEE PAGE 108)
2 tbsp OLIVE OIL, PLUS MORE
   FOR GREASING
1 ONION, FINELY CHOPPED
350 g/ 12 oz MUSHROOMS, SLICED
2 GARLIC CLOVES, CRUSHED
2 tbsp CHOPPED PARSLEY
2 tbsp DOUBLE CREAM
6 SLICES OF CORN BREAD (SEE PAGE
   16), ABOUT 2 cm/ ¾ in THICK
6 SMALL GOATS' CHEESES OR SLICES
   OF GOATS' CHEESE (SEE ABOVE)
SALT AND PEPPER

Soak the dried mushrooms for 30 minutes in 150 ml/¼ pt hot water. Drain, reserving the soaking liquid and straining it through muslin or a coffee filter to remove any grit. Chop the soaked mushrooms.

Heat the olive oil in a saucepan over a moderate heat and fry the onion for 5–10 minutes, stirring frequently, until soft and translucent.

Add the sliced mushrooms, the garlic and parsley and continue to cook, stirring occasionally, for another 5 minutes or until the mushrooms begin to soften. Add the chopped dried mushrooms and their soaking liquid, season with salt and pepper and simmer 2–3 minutes more. Stir in the cream and remove from the heat.

Preheat the oven to 200C/400F/gas6 and grease a baking sheet with oil.

Using a pastry cutter, cut as large a circle as is possible from each of the corn bread slices. Arrange these on the prepared baking sheet. Top each with a cheese or slice of cheese and bake for about 5 minutes, or until the cheese is hot and just melting.

Meanwhile, if necessary, reheat the mushroom mixture without allowing it to boil.

To serve: place a cheese-topped corn bread slice on each of 6 warmed plates and spoon the mushroom ragout next to it. Serve at once.

AVOCADO AND WALNUT RISOTTO

Avocado pears are almost always eaten raw, but they are just as delicious hot. Here their mild flavour and smooth texture contrast with the sharp taste of Parmesan cheese and the crunch of walnuts in a creamy risotto.

The ingredients are far from traditional, but the method of cooking the risotto is quite classic, and will not be completely successful unless you use an Italian risotto rice such as arborio, which is available from delicatessens and large supermarkets.

This risotto should not need extra seasoning as the stock will give it enough flavour and the Parmesan is itself quite salty.

2 tbsp EXTRA VIRGIN OLIVE OIL
1 LARGE ONION, CHOPPED
3 GARLIC CLOVES, CRUSHED
425 g/ 15 oz RISOTTO RICE
   (SEE ABOVE)
ABOUT 1.75 litres/ 3 pt STOCK
150 ml/ ¼ pt WHITE WINE
85 g/ 3 oz FRESHLY GRATED
   PARMESAN CHEESE
2 RIPE AVOCADOS
55 g/ 2 oz CHOPPED WALNUTS
2 tbsp CHOPPED PARSLEY

Heat the oil in a large heavy-based saucepan over a moderate heat and cook the onion, stirring, for about 5 minutes or until translucent.

Add the garlic and rice and stir-fry for 2–3 minutes, or until each grain of rice is coated with oil and begins to look translucent.

In another pan, bring the stock to the boil and leave it on a very low heat to simmer gently.

Pour the wine over the rice and cook over a moderate heat, stirring constantly, until all the liquid has evaporated.

Ladle enough of the simmering stock over the rice barely to cover it. Cook over a moderate heat, stirring occasionally, until all the liquid has been absorbed.

Continue in this way for 20–25 minutes, until all the stock has been used up and the rice is tender. The finished risotto should be quite wet and creamy, but with a little 'bite' left in the centre of each grain. If all the stock is used up before the rice is cooked, add a little boiling water instead.

Just before the rice is fully cooked, stir in half the Parmesan.

At the last minute, peel and dice the avocados, discarding the stones. Fold this gently into the rice mixture together with the walnuts.

To serve: pile the risotto on hot dishes or plates, scatter over the remaining Parmesan and sprinkle with parsley.

VERY GREEN SALAD WITH HERB VINAIGRETTE

This is an idea or inspiration rather than an exact recipe. Use your imagination, and whatever top-quality green vegetables and salad leaves are available. I might use mixed leaves including lettuce, rocket and watercress, lightly cooked asparagus, green and broad beans, celery and avocado.

To 4 tablespoons of Vinaigrette (see page 18), add 1–2 tablespoons of whatever fresh herbs are available (except sage and rosemary, which are too strongly flavoured and not nice eaten raw).

Toss the salad mixture in this dressing.

CAPPUCCINO ICE-CREAM

I first encountered an ice-cream served in this way at the Four Seasons Restaurant of London's Inn on the Park Hotel, where Bruno Loubet – one of the greatest chefs of our time – cooks simply perfect food. This is my version, which is incredibly quick and easy.

If you don't have enough coffee cups that you dare put in the freezer, freeze the ice-cream in small heat-proof glass bowls (or one big one).

Make chocolate shavings by pulling a swivel vegetable peeler across the top of a block of cold dark chocolate.

Makes 1.1 litres/ 2 pt
6 EGG YOLKS (SAVE THE WHITES TO MAKE THE PAVLOVA ON PAGE 53)
4 heaped tsp **INSTANT COFFEE GRANULES**
55 g/ 2 oz **SUGAR**
300 ml/ ½ pt **DOUBLE CREAM, WHIPPED UNTIL STIFF**
To serve
150 ml/ ¼ pt **WHIPPING CREAM, WHIPPED TILL FOAMY BUT NOT STIFF**
CHOCOLATE POWDER (COCOA OR DRINKING CHOCOLATE) OR CHOCOLATE FLAKES OR SHAVINGS (SEE ABOVE)

Place the egg yolks in a bowl and, using an electric whisk, whisk them for 2–3 minutes or until they are light and fluffy. (You can make this ice-cream with a hand whisk, but it will take twice as long – so find a volunteer to help and take it in turns as your arms get tired!).

Put 125 ml/4 fl oz water, the coffee granules and sugar in a small pan and heat until the water is almost boiling and the coffee and sugar are dissolved.

Pour this mixture over the beaten egg yolks in a thin steady stream, while whisking vigorously. Continue to whisk until the mixture is cool, has increased considerably in volume and is as thick and foamy as whipped cream. (This might take up to 4–5 minutes.)

Fold in the stiffly whipped cream and pour the mixture into large tea or coffee cups (see above). Freeze for at least 8 hours before serving.

Take the ice-cream from the freezer 4–5 minutes before serving. Place the cups on saucers with teaspoons. Spoon over the whipped cream and sprinkle lightly with chocolate powder, chocolate flakes or shavings.

Fast Start

In this special-occasion menu, cheese plays an all-important role – appearing at the beginning and the end of the meal. The unusual last course and the fabulous-looking main course both require some time and effort in the kitchen, but the spectacular first course – which will impress the most sophisticated gourmet – takes only moments to prepare and just 3 minutes to cook!

DANIELLE'S GRILLED GORGONZOLA IN LEAF PARCELS

TART OF STUFFED TOMATOES IN PESTO CUSTARD BEETROOT, RED ONION AND PINE KERNEL SALAD

WARM GOATS' CHEESE MOUSSE WITH WALNUTS AND LAVENDER HONEY

DANIELLE'S GRILLED GORGONZOLA IN LEAF PARCELS

As a food writer I am lucky enough occasionally to be taken out for lunch to the latest trendy restaurants by young PR women. One such 'media glamourpuss' (her words!) who is always in touch with the latest trends in fashionable food gave me this wonderfully simple recipe. Do serve a good tasty bread, like Italian ciabatta, to mop up the juices.

Torta di Gorgonzola is an Italian speciality cheese made from layers of fresh Gorgonzola sandwiched with creamy Mascarpone. It is available from delicatessens and good cheese counters. This recipe is also good made with a creamy goats' cheese and large radicchio leaves work even better than lettuce.

3 SLICES OF TORTA DI
  GORGONZOLA, ABOUT 1–2.5 cm/
  ½–1 in THICK OR 6 SMALL FRESH
  GOATS' CHEESES OR 6 SLICES
  FROM A LONG LOG
115 g/ 4 oz SUN-DRIED TOMATOES IN
  OIL, DRAINED (RESERVING THE
  OIL) AND COARSELY CHOPPED
6 LARGE COS LETTUCE LEAVES
3 tbsp EXTRA VIRGIN OLIVE OIL
55 g/ 2 oz FRESHLY GRATED
  PARMESAN CHEESE
55 g/ 2 oz PINE KERNELS
BLACK PEPPER
FRESH BASIL LEAVES, TO GARNISH

Chill the slices of cheese for at least 30 minutes. If using Torta, cut each slice in half to give 6 square pieces.

Preheat a hot grill and grease the grill pan with the oil from the sun-dried tomatoes.

Gently pull the wrinkles out of the lettuce leaves and wrap each piece of cheese in one. Place the parcels in the oiled grill pan, seam side down.

Brush the parcels with some of the olive oil and sprinkle them with Parmesan and pine kernels. Drizzle them with the remaining oil and add a good twist of black pepper.

Place under the preheated grill for about 3 minutes, until the Parmesan and nuts are browned but not cremated.

Using a fish slice, transfer the parcels to 6 warmed plates. Surround them with sun-dried tomatoes and garnish with basil leaves. Serve immediately.

LEFT: *Tart of Stuffed Tomatoes in Pesto Custard (page 120);* RIGHT: *Danielle's Grilled Gorgonzola in Leaf Parcels*

TART OF STUFFED TOMATOES IN PESTO CUSTARD

Inspired once more by an Australian recipe, this spectacular-looking tart takes a little time to prepare, but is not difficult and is well worth the effort.

Ready-made Italian pesto sauce, made from basil, garlic and pine kernels, is available in jars from supermarkets and delicatessens.

9 EQUAL SIZED TOMATOES
  (WEIGHING ABOUT 675 g/ 1½ lb
  IN TOTAL)
225 g/ 8 oz SHORTCRUST PASTRY
  (SEE PAGE 18), ROLLED OUT
  THINLY
1 EGG WHITE, LIGHTLY BEATEN
1 tbsp CORNFLOUR
300 ml/ ½ pt MILK
2 EGGS, LIGHTLY BEATEN
1 tbsp PESTO SAUCE (SEE ABOVE)
1 tbsp EXTRA VIRGIN OLIVE OIL
1 ONION, FINELY CHOPPED
55 g/ 2 oz FINE BREADCRUMBS
55 g/ 2 oz GRATED GRUYÈRE
  CHEESE
1 tbsp CHOPPED FRESH HERBS
  OF CHOICE
SALT AND PEPPER

Slice a small 'cap' off the stalk end of each tomato, scoop out and discard the seeds and juice and the caps (or add them to a soup or the stockpot).

Dry the insides of the tomato shells with a clean cloth, then sprinkle lightly with salt. Leave them upturned on a clean cloth or several layers of paper towels to drain for 1 hour. Dry inside again at the end of this time.

Preheat the oven to 190C/375F/gas5.

Line a 23 cm/9 in loose-bottomed flan tin with the pastry and bake blind for 10 minutes. Brush with beaten egg white and return to the oven for 3 more minutes. This will give a 'waterproof' coat to the pastry shell, so that it remains crisp after the filling is added.

Mix the cornflour to a paste with a little of the milk, then whisk in the rest of the milk with the eggs and the pesto. Season with salt and pepper.

Heat the oil in a frying pan over a low to moderate heat and stir fry the onion for 5–10 minutes, until soft and translucent. Remove the pan from the heat and allow it to cool a little. Then mix in the breadcrumbs, grated cheese and herbs and season well with salt and pepper. Use this mixture to stuff the tomatoes.

Pour the custard mixture into the pastry shell. Then arrange the tomatoes, stuffing side up, in the custard, keeping it as neat looking as possible.

Bake for about 30 minutes, or until the custard is set. Serve hot, warm or cold.

BEETROOT, RED ONION AND PINE KERNEL SALAD

In my view, beetroot is a much underrated vegetable. Its mild sweet flavour marries very well with those of other ingredients in mixed salads like this one, which looks as good as it tastes. Pine kernels are available from some supermarkets and delicatessens, but chopped walnuts would make a good alternative in this recipe.

350 g/ 12 oz COOKED
  BEETROOT, SLICED
2 RED ONIONS, THINLY SLICED
55 g/ 2 oz PINE KERNELS
4 tbsp VINAIGRETTE (SEE PAGE 18)
½ tsp CARAWAY SEEDS
1 tbsp CHOPPED PARSLEY
  OR CHIVES

Grease 6 small ramekin dishes or other suitable heatproof moulds with melted butter.

Thoroughly mix the cheese (including the soft white furry skin) with the eggs and cream in a blender or food processor. (This can be done by hand but you must first thoroughly soften the cheese by beating with a wooden spoon, before mixing in the eggs and cream, and the end result should be pushed through a sieve to eliminate any offending lumps.)

Divide the mixture between the moulds and smooth the tops. Cover each tightly with a little disc of foil. (The mousses can be prepared in advance up to this stage and kept in the refrigerator for up to 6 hours.)

The mousses can be cooked in 2 ways: either in a bain-marie, or deep roasting pan half filled with hot water, in an oven preheated to 190C/375F/gas5 for about 25 minutes; or in a covered steamer over simmering water for about 35 minutes. (I use a Chinese bamboo steamer over a wok.) Either way, they are ready to serve when they are just set.

To serve: turn the mousses out on warmed plates, drizzle 1 tablespoon of honey over each and scatter them with walnut pieces.

Tart of Stuffed Tomatoes in Pesto Custard

Arrange the sliced beetroot and onions in a shallow dish and scatter over the pine kernels.

Mix the vinaigrette with the caraway seeds and then drizzle this over the salad. Leave for about 1 hour at room temperature to allow the flavours to develop.

Sprinkle over the chopped herbs just before serving.

WARM GOATS' CHEESE MOUSSE WITH WALNUTS AND LAVENDER HONEY

This recipe might sound like a rather odd combination, but I think it's quite stunning. It was inspired by a delicious meal I enjoyed in the Languedoc. To finish, we were served pure white rounds of soft fresh goats' cheese drizzled with local honey.

450 g/ 1 lb SOFT GOATS' CHEESE

2 EGGS, LIGHTLY BEATEN

4 tbsp DOUBLE CREAM

6 tbsp LAVENDER HONEY (OR THE
   BEST FLOWER HONEY YOU
   CAN FIND)

55 g/ 2 oz CHOPPED WALNUTS

MELTED BUTTER, FOR GREASING

The Italian Job

The Italian culinary repertoire is perhaps, for me, the one which celebrates the pleasures of eating vegetables more than any other. What imagination and variety is shown in the countless recipes producing delicious and satisfying dishes with neither meat nor fish! Serve this menu to anyone and they will certainly know they have enjoyed an Italian meal, but they probably won't even notice it was a vegetarian one!

'SANDWICHES' OF BAKED AUBERGINE WITH GRILLED PEPPERS AND MOZZARELLA

PENNE WITH GOATS' CHEESE, SPINACH, BROAD BEANS AND PEAS ORANGE, OLIVE AND ONION SALAD

TIRAMISU

DANIELLE'S GRILLED GORGONZOLA IN LEAF PARCELS

As a food writer I am lucky enough occasionally to be taken out for lunch to the latest trendy restaurants by young PR women. One such 'media glamourpuss' (her words!) who is always in touch with the latest trends in fashionable food gave me this wonderfully simple recipe. Do serve a good tasty bread, like Italian ciabatta, to mop up the juices.

Torta di Gorgonzola is an Italian speciality cheese made from layers of fresh Gorgonzola sandwiched with creamy Mascarpone. It is available from delicatessens and good cheese counters. This recipe is also good made with a creamy goats' cheese and large radicchio leaves work even better than lettuce.

3 SLICES OF TORTA DI GORGONZOLA, ABOUT 1–2.5 cm/ ½–1 in THICK OR 6 SMALL FRESH GOATS' CHEESES OR 6 SLICES FROM A LONG LOG
115 g/ 4 oz SUN-DRIED TOMATOES IN OIL, DRAINED (RESERVING THE OIL) AND COARSELY CHOPPED
6 LARGE COS LETTUCE LEAVES
3 tbsp EXTRA VIRGIN OLIVE OIL
55 g/ 2 oz FRESHLY GRATED PARMESAN CHEESE
55 g/ 2 oz PINE KERNELS
BLACK PEPPER
FRESH BASIL LEAVES, TO GARNISH

Chill the slices of cheese for at least 30 minutes. If using Torta, cut each slice in half to give 6 square pieces.

Preheat a hot grill and grease the grill pan with the oil from the sun-dried tomatoes.

Gently pull the wrinkles out of the lettuce leaves and wrap each piece of cheese in one. Place the parcels in the oiled grill pan, seam side down.

Brush the parcels with some of the olive oil and sprinkle them with Parmesan and pine kernels. Drizzle them with the remaining oil and add a good twist of black pepper.

Place under the preheated grill for about 3 minutes, until the Parmesan and nuts are browned but not cremated.

Using a fish slice, transfer the parcels to 6 warmed plates. Surround them with sun-dried tomatoes and garnish with basil leaves. Serve immediately.

LEFT: *Tart of Stuffed Tomatoes in Pesto Custard (page 120)*; RIGHT: *Danielle's Grilled Gorgonzola in Leaf Parcels*

'SANDWICHES' OF BAKED AUBERGINE WITH GRILLED PEPPERS AND MOZZARELLA

The wonderful combination of flavours in this spectacular, but simple-to-make, starter will bring a sunny taste of the Mediterranean to your table. I sometimes make it with soft fresh goats' cheeses (one small cheese, split in two, per person).

2 tbsp **OLIVE OIL, PLUS MORE FOR GREASING**
2 **LONG NARROW AUBERGINES, CUT ACROSS INTO 18 THICK SLICES**
3 **RED SWEET PEPPERS**
2 **TOMATOES, FINELY CHOPPED**
4 tbsp **VINAIGRETTE (SEE PAGE 18)**
2 **MOZZARELLA CHEESES, CUT INTO A TOTAL OF 12 SLICES**
SALT AND PEPPER
WATERCRESS SPRIGS, TO GARNISH

Preheat the oven to 220C/425F/gas7 and grease a baking sheet with some oil.

Sprinkle the aubergine slices with salt and leave them for 30 minutes in a colander to allow any bitter juices to be drawn out. Rinse thoroughly and pat dry with paper towels.

Brush the aubergine slices on one side with olive oil. Season them with salt and pepper and arrange them in a single layer, greased side up, on the prepared baking sheet.

Bake for 10–15 minutes, or until completely soft and golden brown. Remove from the oven and allow to cool.

Meanwhile, cut the peppers in quarters and remove the seeds. Place the pepper quarters, skin side up, in a single layer in a grill pan and grill them until all the skin is blackened. Put them in a plastic bag and allow them to cook in their own steam for 5 minutes. Then remove the blackened skin.

Add the chopped tomatoes to the vinaigrette dressing.

Make 'sandwiches' using 3 slices of aubergine per portion with a slice of cheese and a slice of pepper between each of the aubergine layers.

Arrange the 'sandwiches' on 6 plates, pour over the dressing and garnish with watercress sprigs.

PENNE WITH GOATS' CHEESE, SPINACH, BROAD BEANS AND PEAS

600 g/ 1 lb 5 oz PENNE (OR OTHER
    PASTA SHAPE OF CHOICE)
175 ml/ 6 fl oz EXTRA VIRGIN OLIVE
    OIL
115 g/ 4 oz CHUNK OF PARMESAN CHEESE
225 g/ 8 oz TRIMMED SPINACH LEAVES
140 g/ 5 oz COOKED PEAS
140 g/ 5 oz COOKED BROAD BEANS
400 g/ 14 oz GOATS' CHEESE,
    CRUMBLED INTO CHERRY-SIZED
    PIECES
3 tbsp CHOPPED PARSLEY
SALT AND PEPPER

Cook the pasta in boiling salted water according to the instructions on the packet, until tender but still firm. Drain and pour in 2 tablespoons of the oil. Toss well to coat the pasta thoroughly in the oil.

While the pasta is cooking, pare the Parmesan with a swivel-bladed vegetable peeler to make it into shavings.

Heat the remaining oil in a large saucepan or wok. When really hot, add the spinach and stir-fry for 10 seconds. Add the peas and beans and stir-fry for 10 more seconds.

Add the cooked pasta and the goats' cheese. Season well with salt and pepper. Toss well together over the heat for another 10 seconds and then serve immediately in warmed plates or dishes, sprinkled with the Parmesan shavings and parsley.

ORANGE, OLIVE AND ONION SALAD

This great combination of flavours makes a salad which is perfect to serve as a light starter, a side salad or as part of a buffet meal. Any kind of small oranges will do, but use satsumas when in season as they are so easy to peel. Any mild onion will do, but use red ones if you see them, as they produce a particularly pretty salad.

6 SATSUMAS (SEE ABOVE), PEELED
    AND THINLY SLICED
2 SMALL ONIONS (SEE ABOVE),
    THINLY SLICED
36 BLACK OLIVES
4 tbsp VINAIGRETTE (SEE PAGE 18)
FEW SALAD LEAVES, TO GARNISH

Put the onion and orange slices and the olives in a bowl. Pour over the dressing and toss gently but thoroughly.

Divide between 6 plates and garnish with salad leaves.

TIRAMISU

Tiramisu seems to be one of the trendiest puddings of the moment, taking over where zabaglione left off. There are as many variations as there are restaurants which serve it. This is the best recipe I have tasted and it is also wonderfully easy to make. It comes from an excellent Italian restaurant in South London called Osteria Antica Bologna.

4 EGGS, SEPARATED
4 tbsp ICING SUGAR
3 tbsp BRANDY
500 g/ 1 lb 2 oz MASCARPONE
    CHEESE
ABOUT 18 SAVOYARDE BISCUITS
    (ALSO CALLED LADIES' FINGERS OR
    BOUDOIR BISCUITS)
ABOUT 300 ml/ ½ pt VERY STRONG
    FRESHLY MADE COFFEE, COOLED
3 tbsp COCOA POWDER

Whisk the egg yolks with the sugar until pale and fluffy. Then whisk in the brandy followed by the cheese.

Whisk the egg whites until very stiff and then fold these into the cheese mixture.

In a deep serving bowl (glass if possible), spread one-third of the cheese mixture in the bottom. Now make a layer of biscuits, dipping each one briefly in the coffee first (long enough for them to be soaked, but not too long or they will disintegrate – I find counting 'one and', as you dip them in, just the right length of time). Break the biscuits in half, if necessary, to fit the corners.

Continue with a layer of another third of the cheese mixture, followed by the other half of the biscuits and finish with the remaining cheese mixture. (So in all there should be 5 layers: 3 of cheese mixture, sandwiching 2 of biscuits dipped in coffee.) Smooth the top and sprinkle over the cocoa.

I like to make this dish in advance and then chill it for a couple of hours before serving it. If doing this, it is better to wait until the last moment to sprinkle on the cocoa.

INDEX